LEVELING UP

ERIC SIU

Foreword by HOWARD MARKS
FOUNDER OF ACTIVISION

LEVELING UP

How to Master the Game of Life

●● **PAGE TWO** BOOKS

Every reasonable effort has been made to contact the
copyright holders for work reproduced in this book.
The Ladders of Wealth Creation concept was created
by ConvertKit founder Nathan Barry.

Cataloguing in publication information is
available from Library and Archives Canada.
ISBN 978-1-989603-53-6 (hardcover)
ISBN 978-1-989603-54-3 (ebook)

Page Two
www.pagetwo.com

Edited by James Harbeck
Copyedited by Crissy Calhoun
Proofread by Alison Strobel
Jacket and interior design by Taysia Louie
Jacket and chapter opening illustrations
by Marie Bergeron
Additional graphics by Taysia Louie
Printed and bound in Canada by Friesens
Distributed in Canada by Raincoast Books
Distributed in the US and internationally by
Publishers Group West, a division of Ingram

21 22 23 24 25   5 4 3 2 1

LevelingUp.com

This book is dedicated to all the gamers who don't think they can. **Trust me, you can.**

CONTENTS

FOREWORD

MOST PEOPLE KNOW Activision Blizzard as the company that put forth titles such as *Call of Duty*, *Quake*, *Warcraft*, *StarCraft*, and more. What people don't know is its origin story: how I bought the company out of bankruptcy to help build it into the number-one gaming company in the world.

In the early days, no one would work with Activision: we couldn't hire because we were bankrupt, Walmart wanted to have nothing to do with us, and even Walt Disney didn't see us as a "real business." With the resilience of our team, we slowly turned the ship around. I eventually left the company, before the Blizzard merger, and decided to try my hand again by buying Acclaim (known for *Mortal Kombat*, NBA *Jam*, and more).

I'm willing to bet that many of you think that kind of success story would never apply to you—I was that way before, too. And I'm here to tell you that you couldn't be more wrong; all you have to do is to find the right information and continue to level up.

That's where Eric Siu comes into the picture. I met Eric when I was just starting to build my crowdfunding platform, StartEngine, and I was intrigued by his mission to level up the entire world. Most successful entrepreneurs don't realize all the steps they had to take to achieve success, and by the time they reach it, they've forgotten the playbook and it's difficult to pass down practical advice to aspiring individuals who want to take the next step.

Thankfully, Eric has put together a playbook for all gamers to help them become the best versions of themselves and make a positive impact on the world. This is the book I wish I had growing up and I'm positive that it will help you level up to accomplish your wildest dreams.

Howard Marks,
founder of Activision

INTRODUCTION

JUST HOW BIG is gaming around the world?

As of August 2019, 2.6 *billion* people were playing games. Amazon bought online streaming service Twitch for $970 million. Tencent paid over $400 million for *League of Legends* creator Riot Games. Activision Blizzard bought *Candy Crush* publisher King for $5.9 billion.

Entire stadiums fill up with fans for gaming championships there just to *watch* competitors play computer games. Add in the fact that these championships are streamed, and we're talking about numbers bigger than American football or basketball. The *League of Legends* championship in 2018 alone accounted for 100 million unique viewers. *Minecraft* YouTube sensation Jordan Maron (known as CaptainSparklez) bought a $4.5 million mansion in Los Angeles.

All of this would've been hard to believe in the 1990s, but gaming is now very much a reality baked into our lives. Celebrities regularly talk about gaming. Mega entrepreneur

Elon Musk (CEO of Tesla and SpaceX, cofounder of PayPal and of SolarCity) responded to a Reddit thread with his favorite video games, showing their positive impact on his life. One thing is for sure: gaming has finally reached the masses—and it isn't going away any time soon.

My Backstory

My name is Eric Siu and I'm an entrepreneur who helps other businesses grow. I have a marketing agency that has served companies like Amazon, Nordstrom, Salesforce, and Uber. I also run a marketing analytics company called ClickFlow.

On my weekly podcast, *Leveling Up*, I interview world-class entrepreneurs about personal and business growth. I have another podcast, *Marketing School*, where I nerd out on marketing with my cohost, Neil Patel, every single day.

I regularly contribute to publications such as *Entrepreneur*, *Forbes*, *Fast Company*, and more. I'm a proud member of both Entrepreneurs' Organization (EO) and Young Presidents' Organization (YPO), which are modern-day business "guilds" that help you get ahead.

Before all the business-y stuff, I was a hardcore gamer. I spent my time playing *World of Warcraft*, *EverQuest*, *Defense of the Ancients*, *Counter-Strike*, *Quake*, Team Fortress, *Warcraft III*, *Diablo*, and many others. Whenever I had to log off, I would dream about taking the excitement of playing games to the real world—somehow.

Why? Because I accomplished so much more in games than I did in real life. In games, I won championships, played with the best teams, and accomplished the toughest feats that most people could only dream of. In the gaming world, I felt like I was contributing to something bigger than myself and I felt connected to others. Not so much in real life. I was constantly written off and had little confidence in myself.

I'm not telling you about what I've done to brag about my success. I'm telling you all this because if you approach life as a game, as I have, you'll achieve success and eventually be able to play the ultimate game: business.

And I really mean that. In fact, I think success is inevitable if you develop the mindsets and habits taught in this book— just look at them as power-ups that make you stronger.

And in case you had any doubts, it's a game that *anyone* can play. Why do I say that? Because I almost got kicked out of high school and college, I was never good at dating, and I was seen by my parents and my peers as someone who "didn't have anything going for him." But somehow I made it work.

If I can do it, you can do it.

That's why I'm writing this book: for you, the gamer with big aspirations, the hero.

The Beginning

Growing up, I was a disappointment in the eyes of my parents. I never cared much for school and I was terrible at sports. In fact, I was almost always chosen last when it came to pickup games. School never made much sense to me because having to wake up, report to someone, and obey a regime based on what others thought I should learn didn't sit well with me. I wanted to do things on my own terms.

I wanted to be free.

Thankfully, when I was five, my mom took me to a local Toys'R'Us to buy a Super Nintendo console that came with *Street Fighter II* and *Super Mario World*. It was a pivotal moment in my life.

I was instantly hooked by the storylines and graphics: from fighting M. Bison in *Street Fighter* to flying around with my yellow cape in *Super Mario World*. I was overcome by feelings of, well, ecstasy. Temporarily suspending all of my real-life worries (yes, five-year-old boys have worries, too) to attain my in-game goals is a feeling I'll cherish forever.

As I grew older, I started to notice something at school: the better I got at games, the more I was able to relate with the "cool" kids. The possibility of elevating my social status in high school drove me to work at gaming even harder. Obviously, if you were an elite player, you were considered "cool." For the first time in my life, I realized that gaming drove me to improve. It gave me a burning desire to be exceptional.

Even girls at school had to accept the fact that games were "cool" because that's what the boys liked to do. And what better way to get a boy's attention than to be a part of the growing gaming phenomenon? I even remember a small group of girls going to PC cafés to play games with the guys because they wanted to get their attention.

Today, plenty of girls play games and broadcast their livestreams on Twitch and boys *idolize* these young women. Oh, how times have changed. We live in an age where being a nerd is cool, and I'm confident in saying that without gaming, I would not be where I am today. I always thought that if real life were a game, I would excel at it no matter what. If I could somehow just carry over my gaming mentality, then success would be virtually guaranteed.

Today, that game for me is business.

Now, let me tell you about who this book is for and what it will do for you. This book is for you *if*:

- You are interested in crafting your own path in life
- You value your personal freedom
- You have trouble doing what you're told to do "just because it's always been done that way"
- You were never really interested in school
- You were considered "below average" by your peers
- You will do anything it takes to succeed
- You understand that getting good at something takes hard work and practice
- You study hard at the subjects you're interested in
- You have always wanted to train with the best and fight against the best
- You are willing to collaborate with others to achieve big dreams
- You want to live your life to its fullest potential

This book is *not* for you if:

- You are looking to achieve fame (although that naturally comes if you are successful)
- You want to make a quick buck
- You aren't willing to put in the sweat equity to move ahead of the pack

- You think your fate is predetermined

- You don't think you can grow any more

- You want to coast for the rest of your life

This book will:

- Reveal the key traits relating to gaming and life success

- Show you what you can do to start to achieve business success

- Provide bite-sized nuggets of insight for you to act on

- Give you specific examples of how gaming paved the way for business leaders to found multi-million- to billion-dollar companies like Activision Blizzard

- Provide additional insights from *Leveling Up* podcast guests to prove that *anybody* can win in business and life

- Give you quests that will show you a way to game your way to success

Most importantly, this book will help you build the right mindset to accomplish incredible things in your life that you previously thought were impossible.

Throughout the book, I will continue to reinforce the concept of "life gamification." The idea of life gamification is that you are viewing your life through the lens of a game. Keep in mind that I might mention games that you are unfamiliar with and that's totally fine; it's the principles from this book that matter.

It's fun to wake up in the morning when you're on a meaningful quest for self-improvement, collecting helpful power-ups. The more power-ups you collect, the faster you will level up and the stronger you, the hero, will become.

You will find special passcodes at the ends of certain chapters that lead to an exciting bonus at the end of the book. When you finish collecting all the special passcodes, you will unlock a memorable framework to help you grow for the long term. *Caution: you must finish the book in order to understand and fully benefit from the framework.* Don't say I didn't warn you. :)

Now let's transform your life into a game.

LEVEL

1

NEWBIE STRUGGLES

NEW! Level 1
acquired!

In progress

**"Morning will come,
it has no choice."**

MARTY RUBIN

I HAD JUST FINISHED OFF my opponent in a one-on-one fight to win a championship that crowned me as the top player of my class in *EverQuest*, a massive multiplayer online role-playing game (MMORPG). I had conquered Dharma from our archrival guild, Magna Carta. I wasn't just "Erico" anymore; I was "Erico the Wanderer." People from all over the game sent me private messages congratulating me on my victory. Everyone in my guild was ecstatic because we'd brought home another title that further entrenched us as the number-one team.

In the "real" world of my parents and friends from school, my win didn't mean much. But to my thirteen-year-old self, a nerd who always sucked at sports and never caught the attention of girls, the victory felt major. I hadn't expected to win. I had started out as a newbie with nothing—no ammo, no equipment, no money, and no weapons. I was naked, a peasant, an apprentice at best. Everyone I fought in the tournament had better equipment than I had and was stronger. I was only level 55 while they were all level 60—the highest level possible. But by fighting through tough situations and leveling up, I had surprised myself and won. Getting respect and validation from fellow gamers gave me the confidence that I could accomplish virtually anything in the world.

And, as I found out later, bringing that attitude to my real life helped me pull off bigger things than I ever could have imagined.

My Journey

Before I got serious about gaming, I constantly struggled. My path never really flowed the way my parents wanted it to: they wanted me to get good grades, go to a great college, and get a good job. But their philosophies didn't jibe with me and what I wanted to do: have a good time, on my own terms.

In the real world, the one that mattered to most of the people around me, I was always late to catch on to things. I'd always be chosen last for pickup basketball games. I was at the bottom of the food chain when I joined the high school drumline. I was picked on frequently because I was smaller and shy. I was told to "be cool" or to "stop trying to fit in." I always had trouble summoning up the courage to ask out girls. In fact, I didn't have my first real girlfriend until I was twenty-six. "You're just not good enough to do that stuff," I would constantly tell myself. I had an enormous chip on my shoulder growing up and was hellbent on proving all the naysayers wrong. I tried all kinds of ways, but I just continued to fail over and over. People laughed at me and underestimated me, but I always had my escape: the world of gaming.

In the days before gaming was called eSports, my mom bought five-year-old me that Super Nintendo. I was instantly hooked. I felt I could escape into another world and do amazing things that normal human beings couldn't. From becoming Mario and riding Yoshi to playing *Mario Kart* and *Street Fighter*, there were so many options available to me. From the age of nine, when I got my first computer, I became enamored with the world of *Diablo*, *StarCraft*, *Warcraft*, *EverQuest*, *Command & Conquer*, and more.

When the internet changed gaming, my mind was completely blown by the seemingly infinite possibilities to play with people I'd never met and to make friends with like-minded people. I loved everything about internet gaming: the stories, gameplay, camaraderie, and feeling like I truly belonged to something greater than myself. Gone were the pressures of having to get straight As, date a cute girl, or go to a great college. I got to escape from everything and actually contribute to a cause. Gaming is where I found my solace and my strength.

When I first started to play *EverQuest* (the game that led to *World of Warcraft*) at eleven years old, MMORPGs had just started to take shape as a genre. I was on the frontier of a new gaming trend. I struggled in my early *EverQuest* days and found it hard to succeed at the game. It was fairly complicated for a preteen. And there were many confusing aspects of the game that none of us early adopters yet understood. MMORPGs were still very new, and we were all learning through trial by fire. It took me hours to figure out what my role was, what I needed to do, how to level up, how to get around my city, and more. But I committed myself to learning more about each new game.

What I found out was this: I had to take a licking in the beginning of whatever game I tried. The beginning *always* sucks. It's slow, it's boring, and it's hard to see where things are heading.

But eventually I always did.

The beginning of every game *always* sucks. **It's slow, it's boring, and it's hard to see where things are heading.**

I soon learned that to be at the top of the game, I had to study. I went to websites and printed out pages of maps and put them into a binder. I would *never* do something like that for school.

As I studied and improved on my own, I realized that in order to do the most challenging things in the game, I had to join a team. And these weren't just any teams. These were large teams of fifty, sixty, or more people all vying to accomplish things that nobody else had. I knew I had to gain experience first by joining a top three team.

From there, the challenges and pressures of the game increased tenfold because we all had to be on the same page in terms of communication. One big screwup could cause all of us to fail. For the first time, I understood the pride of representing a team. I realized it must be the type of pride that basketball or soccer teams felt when they played in championship matches.

I eventually became a top-tier player in the number-one high-end raid guild (team) for *EverQuest*. I even became the champion of my class (the best character of my type on the server) when I was in middle school. This was far more significant—at least in my preteen mind—than any academic achievement I could have had. In fact, I had never won any athletic trophies, never made honor roll, never had any other notable achievements.

Unfortunately, my parents neither understood nor cared about my gaming accomplishments. They thought I was going down a black hole and would become a failure. They even went as far as hiding my keyboard or my mouse so I couldn't play. We would frequently have big arguments after which I wouldn't talk to my mom for several weeks. Then it would flip, and I wouldn't talk to my dad for a few weeks. I was so passionate about my gaming life that I nearly came to blows with my dad.

But, hey, at least every time I had a quarrel, whichever parent I was on better terms with fed me Burger King Whoppers after school, so I never starved. I did get a little chubby, though.

When I think back to why I was able to win gaming championships despite the odds, it was because of consistent, hard, painstaking work. There's no way I could have gotten there without progressing methodically and patiently.

I write with a sense of pride when I think back to my gaming days, because these accomplishments provided me with foundational confidence that allowed me to eventually succeed in real life and business. Thanks to that confidence, I was able to parlay my gaming experience into resurrecting two companies, taking over one, starting a software company, speaking internationally, hosting two podcasts with millions of monthly listens (*Marketing School* and *Leveling Up*), hosting a reality video series (also called *Leveling Up*), and guest lecturing at universities on entrepreneurship and marketing.

The Road Ahead

After reaching the pinnacle in *EverQuest* at the age of thirteen, I knew gaming was my purpose. Every human being in the world wants to feel a sense of purpose—a feeling that they are giving back. Up until that point, I had never felt that because I was, in all fairness, a loser. Gaming made me feel like a winner: I could log on and embody my avatar, someone many people looked up to. Gaming allowed me to step into my alter ego.

I sacrificed a lot to become great at the games I played, including a stronger relationship with my parents and admission to a higher-tier college. I gave up on potential chances to play high school sports (more as a benchwarmer but, hey, that still counts!). I put off my dating life. Ironically, I sometimes also sacrificed my own gaming performance when my attention was diverted to another game.

Nonetheless, for the first time in my life, gaming helped me understand the sacrifices that need to be made to reach the pinnacle in anything. Success is always a struggle. And to achieve it, you have to be willing to fail. A lot. And keep going. It doesn't matter what kind of game it is—an RPG, FPS, MMORPG, RTS, or whatever. The best gamers always go through the struggle. The struggle is the growth opportunity that allows breakthroughs in life.

Even though most people think gaming is a waste of time, I found it to be one of the most helpful investments of my life. It shaped my mindset and taught me to think critically. Gaming was the medium I chose to learn how to improve as a human being. People hold sports such as basketball and soccer in high regard because those games have been played for many years and are accepted into our society. Competitive gaming is still a fairly new phenomenon that is slowly being accepted by our culture.

If you find that gaming resonates with you, know that your time investment will pay off handsomely for you. It certainly helped propel me and others into playing the ultimate game of business.

The Newbie Mindset

When Tim Ferriss, bestselling author of *The 4-Hour Workweek*, started his TV show *The Tim Ferriss Experiment*, he required himself to learn a new skill in four days or less for every episode. Skills included poker playing, parkour obstacle-course training, rally car racing, surfing, playing drums, and more. Every single time he tried something new, he was embarrassingly bad.

Still, he was able to power through because he embraced the role of starting fresh in a new endeavor. And that's the kicker: most people aren't willing to go through the embarrassing starts and would rather stay in their own safe havens. They aren't willing to be newbies.

That's why most people end up being most people.

But if you understand that learning new things is a constant process and that the process is the same *every single time*, you can ignore the stigma that comes with being a newbie. You'll be able to play real life as a game.

Getting started is sometimes the hardest part of leveling up. My ultimate promise is to show you how to make that mindset shift, so you can have fun while accomplishing things beyond your wildest dreams. It'll be one of the most fulfilling transformations in your life.

Power-Ups

Perhaps one of the most powerful concepts I learned from gaming is the importance of power-ups. In a video game, these are bonuses you can collect to gather strength. Whether it's Mario eating a mushroom to get stronger in *Super Mario Bros.*

The best gamers always go through the struggle. **The struggle is the growth opportunity that allows breakthroughs in life.**

or warriors getting important weapons and armor in games like *World of Warcraft* or *League of Legends*, power-ups are important because they improve your efficiency and make it easier to achieve your goals. When Mario eats a mushroom, it doubles his resilience; he can now take two hits instead of one. In *Counter-Strike*, an AK-47 shoots at a much faster rate than a pistol, inflicting more damage per second to opponents. Without power-ups, leveling up takes much longer.

Great power-ups can be challenging to attain. In *EverQuest*, each day we had to wait until six p.m. for our entire team to log on so we could get forty to sixty people together to kill one dragon. Once the dragon was killed, it yielded maybe two items (or power-ups). These raids often took hours, sometimes lasting to two or three a.m. on a weeknight. Good players understand the importance of persevering and continuing to acquire power-ups to stay ahead of the curve.

Here's the cool part: power-ups have parallels in the game of life.

In real life, a power-up could be something that enhances your abilities, such a car that goes faster than average or a phone that provides information to you in a few seconds. As long as it is something that enhances your way of life, it can be considered a power-up.

Real life has many different power-ups:

- **Education:** Education and books unlock insights and allow you to learn from the experiences of others and accelerate your own growth. Why should you repeat the mistakes made hundreds of years ago when our ancestors already put in the pain and sacrifice so you could sidestep them? For example, *The Secrets of Power Negotiating* taught me to always aim to create win/win situations in negotiations. Another example is mentorship. I was fortunate enough to be mentored by my now partner, Neil Patel, when I was first learning digital marketing. I talk about mentorship later in the book.

- **Food:** Often taken for granted in the United States, healthy food gives us energy and allows us to function correctly. We all need it. During my *World of Warcraft* days, I learned that living on guacamole burgers, chili cheese fries, and extra-large raspberry iced teas was not ideal for my health.

- **Love:** Being able to love and be loved by people gives you a sense of purpose. Humans are fundamentally social creatures who love to interact with one another. Those who are alone may eventually end up suffering from depression (which is a power-down). In my early college years, I felt alone because attending classes that didn't jibe with me made no sense. I was seen as a failure by my friends and family. But when I entered *World of Warcraft* or *EverQuest*, I never felt more loved because I had a clear direction to accomplish only what the best could do.

- **Competition:** Competition teaches us to work hard and lights a fire under us to keep going. Everything you see around you has sprouted from competition.

The most successful people in life master these power-ups and continue to hone them. Each chapter in this book provides, in essence, a power-up for real life. Don't feel discouraged if you feel you are lacking certain power-ups. Just focus on getting better. Nobody is perfect across the board—I'm not—and you will need to nurture each power-up once you acquire it.

Remember the book is titled *Leveling Up* for a reason. Each chapter gives you a power-up placed strategically to help you get stronger, smarter, or more adventurous. Take each power-up step by step and add new power-ups as you continue your journey and you will be able to keep leveling up. Don't feel that you need to acquire all of them at the same time. There's no shame in taking your time. When you play life as a game, you'll want to stay in it as long as possible.

Bonus power-ups are sprinkled at the ends of certain chapters to provide a framework at the end of the book that you can use to help ensure your long-term success. And to keep you going, there's a Tomb of Knowledge at the end of the book: a store of tools and power-ups for you to use as you continue on your journey.

One more thing: weapons and armor will need to be repaired over time. Power-ups lose their durability, so it's your responsibility to keep sharpening your weapons—otherwise they'll go dull. The same goes for power-ups in your life. You need to put in the effort to keep them strong and steady. Growing up, I frequently dismissed the value of having a healthy diet and regularly exercising. Maybe that's why my mom always called me "fat boy" in Chinese and never relented.

GAMIFY YOUR LIFE WITH THESE POWER TIPS

- To accomplish anything great, you're required to go through struggles.

- Just because you have struggled in the past does not mean you're entitled to anything. To play at the next level, you'll have a new set of struggles.

- Better to think of yourself as a perpetual newbie: someone who lacks entitlement or preconceived biases has an easier time and reaches goals faster.

- Continue to collect power-ups throughout your life. Other people play at higher levels thanks to the power-ups they have collected on their journey.

QUEST: THE BEGINNING

△ **YOUR POWER-UP** △
A fresh worldview

× **QUEST DEADLINE** ×
1 week

THINK ABOUT SOMETHING you've been wanting to do to improve yourself and your life. Maybe it's journaling in the morning, reading for an hour a day, meditating, or learning a new workout. You have to start at the very beginning. This is your introductory quest.

1 Your first challenge is to figure out how to do it.

A No one's going to hand you a magic book with all the instructions. You already have the magic book, and it's huge, and you have to figure out which parts are the instructions you need. The magic book is *the internet*. Search websites. Look for YouTube videos. Find apps.

B Read the sites you found. Watch the videos. Try the apps.

C Decide what approach seems like it will work best for you. Keep a back-up approach in mind in case you're wrong.

2 Your second challenge is to start making it a habit.

A Set an appointment with yourself to work on it every day for a week.

B Record your performance each day.

C See how you're doing at the end of the week. Awful? Hey, you're just starting. Are you getting what you wanted? What's getting in your way? How can you refocus your priorities on this? What will make you enthusiastic?

D Make a plan for staying on track.

That's it. That's the quest. If you've made it through the first week, you've made it through the first level. Your reward is twofold:

1 You will know how to do a new thing.

2 You get to keep working on that new thing and continuously improve. You do *not* get to stop.

Want help with your habits? Get through every chapter and to the end of the book and you'll find a bonus waiting for you.

LEVEL

2

YOUR
MISSION

NEW! Level 2
acquired!

In progress

"The purpose of life is not to be happy. It is to be useful, to be honorable, to be compassionate, to have it make some difference that you have lived and lived well."

RALPH WALDO EMERSON

WHEN I WAS in eighth grade, I was focused on attaining a sword so rare and powerful that only three people out of 4,000 had it in their possession. Why did I want it? Because not only would it make my character stronger, but it had such a unique and rare look that it would elevate my status.

To get the sword, the game took me on a quest that frequently required me to enlist the aid of my team. This often meant calling forty people to help me at odd hours (sometimes in the early morning). I wanted to achieve a higher status so badly that I left my computer speaker volume on high when I went to bed so I would hear the sound of a rare monster that I had to eliminate as part of the quest. It got to a point where I got a fever from overexerting myself just to attain a sword. A virtual sword. Which I eventually got, by the way.

That's the power of having a worthwhile mission.

When I play games, I'm always trying to level up and gain as much experience as possible for one reason: to accomplish things only *the best* can do. Why? My philosophy is if you're going to spend a lot of time on something, go all in. Going all in means investing more, and doing so gives you a sense of purpose.

During my gaming days, leveling up meant different things depending on the game. In *World of Warcraft* (*WoW*), I joined the best guild to destroy the toughest bosses and to be known as part of the top competitive team in player-versus-player (PvP) combat. I ended up on one of the most well-known PvP guilds on not just the server but in *all* of *World of Warcraft*. When I played *EverQuest*, my goal was to join the best guild and become the best in my class on the server. I ended up winning the best of the best tournament, which definitively named me as the best druid. Not only that, I was the lowest-level druid, at level 55, to win the tournament (the highest level was 60 at the time). The guild I was in was number one at the time, and we faced the toughest challenges.

The Amazing Journey

I'm not stating my accomplishments above to brag. Far from that. I'm showing you that having goals and striving toward them can put you on an amazing journey. I struggled mightily to reach success and the only reason I got there was because I gave myself a tangible mission (or goal) to accomplish.

To embark on that journey, you may need to first lay the groundwork, without any promise of reward. When I look at my achievements in *World of Warcraft* and *EverQuest*, the one consistent trend was the amount of effort I put into those games when I first started out. When these games launched, I rushed to the store on the first day, picked up the game, and played as much as possible to get ahead of everyone else. It was a mission to see who could quickly reach the highest level and then form the best team possible.

In *WoW*, I frequently skipped my college classes to play as much as possible to keep up with my buddies. Sometimes, I

Create your own game of life. **A game that you can play and _win_ on your own terms.**

moved my computer from my dorm to their house just to be closer. Once I stayed with my two friends at their house for thirty days straight. We'd play until six a.m. at times, then get fast food, sleep, wake up again, and start the process back up at two p.m.

That's the kind of dedication it takes to be at the top of your game, no matter what you are doing in life.

Was it always healthy? Definitely not. Do I regret it? No, because when you have a quest, sometimes you need to make sacrifices. Just make sure that if you decide to make sacrifices, doing so doesn't affect your wellbeing in the long term.

Real life is no different from games when it comes to completing quests. Unfortunately, many people wander around aimlessly in life and pass away with much regret. Most people don't want to go all in because they don't know *why* they're doing what they're doing. Why do you think you're on this planet? What is your purpose? What is your quest?

Find or Be Found

Sometimes your mission will find you. I didn't know what mine was in high school and I stumbled through my classes. I almost didn't graduate from high school because I nearly failed a required class my senior year. In college, I had six withdraws in my first year and was subject to dismissal. Then I applied to transfer colleges and I got accepted, only to have that rescinded because my GPA fell below the minimum threshold. I eventually got in because I drove six hours on three separate occasions to persuade the chancellor to let me in.

School as a concept didn't make sense to me because I didn't understand the end goal. I didn't understand the mission I was on. In contrast, games gave me a clear objective and something I felt was worth fighting for. Because I understood the quest, my path was clear, and I knew what I needed to do to be successful.

After college, the only job I could find was doing data entry where I was paid slightly above minimum wage. I was so bored I would get to work early just to sleep at my desk. I'd even play online poker before my coworkers arrived because I was so bored. I didn't feel like I had a purpose in life. It felt just like school again.

I had no mission.

Then my friend Christina told me about digital marketing and how I might find it interesting. She was right; I was hooked from the start. Why? Because it was like playing a game. Through Christina, I got an unpaid internship that I combined with my full-time job. I changed my hours for my full-time gig to six a.m. to two p.m. Then I'd work at the internship from 3:30 p.m. until midnight.

I didn't work as hard as I did as an intern because I *had* to, but because I *wanted* to. I felt the same sense of vigor I did when I played games. That's when I knew I had found a new mission worth fighting for.

In the subsequent 365 days, I secured my first four marketing jobs. One year after that, I became a senior manager. A few months after that, I became a VP of marketing for a startup. Shortly after that, I took over a failing company, turned it around, and rode its success to start more companies, launch podcasts and video shows, and speak around the world. Today, my companies are fortunate enough to work with global organizations like Amazon, Uber, Lyft, Nordstrom, and more. Our podcasts get over one million listens per month and our success continues to compound daily.

Mission or No Mission?

See the difference between mission and no mission?

When there's no mission, there's no direction. With a quest, I have a lot more vigor and I put more energy into things because they're purposeful. Life isn't about finding a job or conforming to norms that say you should be a doctor, engineer, or lawyer. There's no rule that says human beings need to sit through a monotonous job for eight hours a day, praying for the weekend to come (while dreading Mondays). That's a limiting life. Life is meant to be enjoyed on your terms.

The key is to make life like a game. Everyone should have a mission they're pursuing. If you're a child, your mission might be to have fun and to make friends. If you're in college, your mission might be to explore opportunities around you and experiment with new things.

Today, I feel like I've leveled up to where I'm playing the game of life and I'm grateful for every single moment. My mission now? To help you create your own game of life. A game that you can play and *win* on your own terms.

GAMIFY YOUR LIFE WITH THESE POWER TIPS

- Having a mission gives you purpose. And with purpose comes the conviction you need to level up to achieve the success that you want.

- A mission is very important to help a company reach its long-term goals. For example, StartEngine cofounder Howard Marks has a personal mission to help every entrepreneur achieve their dreams. It's a very big mission that he's unlikely to accomplish in his lifetime, but that's what a mission is. You don't need to start big, but start with something so you can get going. Under an overarching mission, you can have sub-missions. These can be your quests.

- Conversely, not having a mission puts you in a position where you're living in limbo and life is just passing you by. This is like being a non-player character. In a role-playing game, a non-player character (NPC) plays a supporting role in the players' quests. NPCs have no quest, no real life; they're just puppets. Don't be an NPC. Become the hero.

△ **YOUR POWER-UP** △

The map for a lifetime of finding prizes

✕ **QUEST DEADLINE** ✕

1 day—and then the rest of your life

WHAT IS THE purpose, cause, or belief that inspires you to do what you do?

We're all shaped by our surroundings and experiences. What's important to you? For me, gaming played a pivotal role in shaping me into who I am. It taught me that I loved learning on my own terms. It taught me how to work well with others. It taught me about the importance of collaboration. It taught me to strive to be the best at whatever I put my time into.

How about you? If you don't determine what mission you are on, you'll wander aimlessly and cannot begin your journey of gamifying life. Watch Simon Sinek's TED Talk about the power of "why," one of the most viewed TED Talks. Your "why" is basically your mission.

A mission starts with asking questions. To figure out your "why," ask yourself the following questions and then write down the answers somewhere safe.

1 What do I love? *For example, I love learning.*

2 What am I good at? If you aren't good at anything yet, what do you want to become good at? *For example, I'm good at teaching through podcasts, videos, speaking, and writing.*

3 What does the world need? *For example, I believe that the world needs to provide better access to and incentives for education.*

4 What are some uncompromising beliefs I have? *For example, I believe that people always have room to improve and those who don't die on the inside.*

5 What kind of people do I get along with? What are their traits? *For example, one of the most important traits I look for in an individual is their bias toward growth. And part of growth means learning.*

6 Who are my enemies? What traits do they have in common? *For example, I don't get along with people who blame their circumstances for their results.*

See where I'm going with all this? Determining the right mission to pursue means asking yourself the right questions. Then you can work toward a meaningful aim.

Write down what you think your answers to the questions add up to for your mission. Don't worry if you don't have an all-encompassing mission right now; the key is getting started and evolving your mission as you go.

My ultimate mission is to help every person in the world level up to make a bigger impact. That starts with you!

LEVEL

3

MINDSET

NEW! Level 3
acquired!

In progress

"If you imagine less,
less will be what you
undoubtedly deserve."

DEBBIE MILLMAN

ACCORDING TO CAROL DWECK, author of *Mindset*, there are two different types of mindsets: fixed and growth. For example, you can look at a glass as half empty or half full. Which mindset do you think you have?

Individuals with fixed mindsets—or a half-empty glass—tend to think there isn't much upward mobility or potential in their life. They think their destiny is set and life is out of their hands. Quite often, these people complain about being "unlucky."

Growth, or abundance-minded, individuals—those who label the glass as half full—see the world as a playground for opportunity. If they don't know something, they'll go out there and learn. If they aren't good at something, they'll work hard and practice until they become great.

Growth individuals consistently take the initiative and challenge themselves with quests so they can improve. The better they become, the more doors open to them for more ambitious quests. Eventually they become so good that they can make a massive impact on society.

Is Success Really in the Cards?

Poker is a game that I started playing in my senior year of high school and it's a fine test of someone's mindset. I frequently observed people around me getting flustered because of a bad run of cards, and I saw pros keep their composure through dry spells. The people with a "half-empty glass" mentality attributed all their results to luck and didn't try to improve on their shortcomings. The people with a "half-full glass" mentality reviewed their mistakes and tried to get incrementally better each session.

During my poker days, I used to play for hours on end (sometimes eighteen hours a day), and sometimes I'd go on winning streaks for weeks and feel invincible. Other times, I would lose for weeks on end (sometimes months) and fall into a deep, dark funk.

During my early days of poker, I took a free $25 deposit credit and made it into $2,500 in a span of a few hours after winning a tournament. I won $2,000 more before luck caught up to me. From $25 to $4,500 to $0 in a span of two days. It was heartbreaking.

The problem? I let the winning streak go to my head; I thought I was ready to take on the world. In poker, tilt is when a player is in an emotional state, often frustration, and adopts a less than optimal strategy, usually resulting in the player falling off their A-game. It's basically another version of a downward spiral.

After gaining a little more experience in the poker world, I took a $50 free credit on a site and turned it into $15,000. I was again on fire and thought I couldn't be stopped. After all, I had $10,500 more than the last time. This time, I thought to myself, I would ride my winnings to a $100,000 bankroll. I then took my winnings into a higher-tier game filled with elite players and promptly lost everything I'd earned.

I was furious. I took out credit card offers and maxed them out without even considering the consequences if I couldn't pay the debt. I then proceeded to lose $20,000. I was nineteen years old and that money meant the world to me. Because I was unable to pay the $20,000 back, the debt continued to accrue interest, which meant I ultimately owed way more money.

So, what did I do? Nothing.

I had a "half-empty glass" mentality and was so focused on making more money that I didn't bother to plug any holes in my game before moving on to higher stakes.

To make matters worse, my credit score dropped to 480. For context, your credit score is what lenders use to determine if they want to rent you an apartment, lease you a car, or let you buy a house—in the United States, it can be as high as 850 and an average score is 700. It matters a lot if you're trying to push ahead in the game of life.

I didn't bother fixing my credit score problem for another six years. As a result, I basically became a handicapped gamer in life: I didn't have the same power-ups that people with a decent credit score had. I felt like my life was spiraling out of control. I was short with my friends, ignored phone calls from my parents, and cursed all the players at the table for being "luckier" than me.

Fortunately, I was able to bring my credit score back to over 800 after a few years.

Don't ever
accept it when
**someone tries
to put you
into a box.**

The Mind Game

So, what's the difference between winners and losers in poker? Mindset.

It wasn't until I started studying poker books, forums, videos, and player behavior through software that I realized that as long as I put in the time, I could slowly level up my skill set.

In poker, even if you are the best player in the world, you will lose at some point. It's a foregone conclusion thanks to the math of the game. It's about how you weather the storm, and the first step is controlling your mindset. You cannot control outside factors, but what you *can* control is how you view the obstacle and what you ultimately *do* to move forward.

It's okay if you lose battles because you can always win the war. But if you don't have your mind screwed on correctly, you're screwed no matter what. The same concept applies to real life.

Just look at Bill Gates and the company he created. Microsoft changed the world and the lives of billions of people with the personal computing revolution. Even as a billionaire, Gates continues to make an impact on the world with the Bill & Melinda Gates Foundation. Many people don't know that Bill's growth mindset was a big factor in why Microsoft allowed pirated copies of Windows. In countries where users couldn't afford the software, Gates let it slide because he felt that the net outcome would help humanity grow faster. Instead of trying to protect his profits, he saw the long-term benefit for humanity through a different lens.

But it wasn't always easy for Gates. He battled against Apple cofounder Steve Jobs for supremacy. He battled against IBM. He battled against the U.S. Department of Justice when it accused Microsoft of being a monopoly. He failed at multiple initiatives on his way to success, but he eventually got there.

All because of his growth mindset.

I'm grateful for what poker taught me because it applies directly to real life. In fact, many of the world's most successful entrepreneurs and investors frequently laud poker as a game that correlates well with business and life. As billionaire investor Chamath Palihapitiya wrote on Twitter, "Poker is a great teacher... deal with poker and you learn to deal with financial variance and emotional tilt—basically the life of an entrepreneur."

Poker is what prepared me for the variance of business.

One of the toughest moments I had to deal with in business happened with my marketing agency, Single Grain. Our business provides marketing services to companies around the world and it heavily relied on Google's search engine. One day, Google changed how its search engines worked, and our business was invalidated overnight. The other four partners decided the business was no longer viable and I ended up taking it over. Over the next twelve months, I saw my team size drop all the way down to one person while the revenues fell to record lows. But the mindset of dealing with variance taught me to weather the storm, and we were eventually able to save the company and pivot it into the thriving business it is today.

Think Growth

In *Mindset*, Carol Dweck writes that the "growth mindset is based on the belief that your basic qualities are things you can cultivate through your efforts. Although people may differ in every which way—in their initial talents and aptitudes, interests, or temperaments—everyone can change and grow through application and experience."

In a study of seventh graders in a New York City school, a group of students was divided into two. Half were taught about the stages of memory while the other half received training in the growth mindset and how to apply it to their work. The results were astounding: three times as many students in the growth mindset group showed an increase in effort and motivation compared with the control group.

IMPACT OF A GROWTH MINDSET INTERVENTION

Math Grades Before and After Intervention

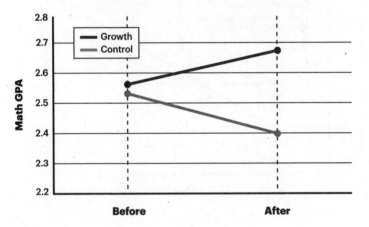

Source: MindsetWorks.com/science/Changing-Mindsets

In another study, a group of fifth graders was divided up to work on a puzzle. After both groups succeeded, one was praised for their effort while the other was praised for their intelligence. The groups reacted differently as more tasks were presented to them. The group praised for their intelligence continued to work on easy tasks while the group praised for their effort proceeded to work on more difficult tasks. In a nutshell, the students who were praised for their effort saw there was room to continually grow while the students praised for their intelligence attributed their success to a fixed quality of themselves.

IMPACT OF PRAISE ON RESILIENCE AFTER FAILURE

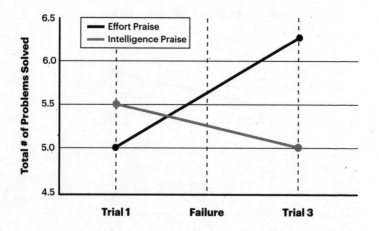

Source: MindsetWorks.com/science/Teacher-Practices

When I was growing up, my parents told me that I wasn't good at math and was not meant for sports, and that I just had to deal with that. Of course, as a child, I believed everything my parents told me because they cared for me and I looked up to them. After going through countless experiences and looking at studies like these, I've learned that my parents grew up in a fixed mindset culture. And that's not their fault; that's just how they were brought up. Don't ever accept it when someone tries to put you into a box.

Twenty-three-time Olympic gold medal winner Michael Phelps wasn't the best swimmer growing up. NBA legend Michael Jordan, known as the greatest basketball player of all time, didn't even make the varsity team on his first try in high school. Imagine if either of them had had a fixed mindset, believing that they couldn't get better. Do you think they would have achieved anywhere near the level of success that they did? Of course not! Having a growth mindset helped contribute to their success.

For every Michael Phelps or Michael Jordan in the world, there are hundreds of thousands of people who live an average life because they don't think they can do otherwise.

Don't be one of them.

GAMIFY YOUR LIFE WITH THESE POWER TIPS

The one thing you have full control of is your attitude. Here are some things you can do to keep your game perspective on life.

- If something isn't going well for you, ask yourself, "Am I performing to the best of my ability right now?" On the rare occasions when I play poker nowadays, I'll ask myself this question, and if the answer is no, I'll rack up my chips and leave.

- Think about the times when you've fallen into a hole that seemed to get deeper and deeper. What was your mindset at the time? How can you change that moving forward?

- Try using the mobile app Headspace or Calm for at least ten days to learn how meditation helps you achieve the right mindset.

- Read DailyStoic.com and subscribe to its email list—it will teach you how to get your mind right and how to deal with the stresses of the world.

- My mobile phone wallpaper says, "Grateful 24/7/365," a mantra from Gary Vaynerchuk. I highly recommend downloading an inspirational mobile wallpaper. You can go to a site like Pinterest or WallpaperPlay.com and search for "inspirational phone wallpapers." It's powerful to constantly reinforce a positive mindset every time you look at your phone. It's a strong power-up, so use it.

- I write in a journal every morning and at the end of the day. At the top, I note three things to be grateful for to set my mind in a positive way. Having that mindset to kick off the day puts me in the mood to go do great things. If you start out the day in a depressed mood versus a positive mood, do you think your work will be better or worse? Go to LevelingUp.com to get a template for your journal.

QUEST: BUILD A POKER MINDSET

1 Take stock of the things you are bad at that you keep trying to be good at.

A What are they? (Math? Sports? Relationships?)

B How much time and energy are you spending on them each week?

c How much are you improving at them?

D What would be the benefit of being better at them?

2 Take stock of the things you are good at.

A What are they? (Sales? Teaching? Poker?)

B Which ones are valuable to you?

c How much time and energy are you spending each week trying to improve at them?

D How much are you improving at them?

3 Determine how much of your week you spend on set 1 that you could be spending on set 2.

A Identify what things you're bad at that you would benefit from being better at and that you have a reasonable hope of improving at.

B Identify whether any of them would repay the effort enough to take time away from things that you're good at and benefit from.

C If there are any, choose one. Allocate enough time each week to improve it significantly, without taking away any time from things you're good at and profit from.

D Draw a line through the rest of set 1. Allocate all the rest of the available time to improving things you're good at and benefit from.

4 Now do it.

Putting that into action completes your initial quest, and you can move up to the next level. *Keeping* it in action is your ongoing challenge. You can't benefit if you don't actually do it.

It's always easier to improve strengths than weaknesses. The key thing to keep in mind is that you can improve anything as long as you put your mind to it. Awareness is the first step.

4

GET
READING

NEW! Level 4
acquired!

In progress

"Live as if you were to die tomorrow. Learn as if you were to live forever."

ISIDORE OF SEVILLE

BILLIONAIRE INVESTOR Warren Buffett and his partner Charlie Munger read at least five hours a day. Buffett once pointed to a stack of nearby books and said to an investing class, "Read 500 pages like this every day. That's how knowledge works. It builds up, like compound interest. All of you can do it, but I guarantee not many of you will do it."

Growing up, I used to believe that reading to learn would end after college. I hated being forced to read things I didn't care about and work on assignments in which I had almost zero interest. Why should someone tell me what I should be reading?

In fact, most people don't read. According to Pew Research, 27 percent of adults surveyed in 2019 said they did not read any books, up from 19 percent in 2011. That's a 42 percent increase!

Who *is* reading? The people who are ahead. Billionaire philanthropist and Microsoft cofounder Bill Gates reads about fifty books a year. Dallas Mavericks owner and billionaire Mark Cuban reads three hours a day and has been doing that since his twenties. Charlie Munger has said, "In my whole life,

I have known no wise people who didn't read all the time—none, zero. You'd be amazed at how much Warren reads—and at how much I read. My children laugh at me. They think I'm a book with a couple of legs sticking out."

The reality of life is that it's an exercise in always learning more. New inventions are sprouting up every day and there are always changes happening in the world. If you're not taking in new information, you're putting yourself at a severe disadvantage.

Elon Musk, who helped start companies such as Tesla and SpaceX, knew *nothing* about sending rockets into space. And yet he figured out how to send rockets up *and* safely back to Earth to be reused. How did he learn? By reading rocket science books, having conversations with some of the smartest rocket scientists, and building an incredible team to help him fulfill his mission.

Know the Game

But we know all this already from gaming. Elite gamers always watch film and learn from their mistakes—just as any professional athlete would. They dissect areas where they make mistakes and try to plug those holes. Coaches provide perspective on blind spots that gamers might have missed—just as in pro sports.

The games I enjoyed and excelled at were those in which I devoted time to learning. In the MMORPG *EverQuest*, I used those printed-out maps to guide me whenever I entered an unfamiliar area. I habitually went to other websites to learn about new item discoveries so I could list out what I wanted to acquire.

I did the same with other MMORPGs. In *Warcraft III* or *StarCraft*, I watched replays after defeats to learn what I could improve. Success can get to your head; that's why I prefer to look at my losses to learn about what I need to fix. As Bill Gates said, "Success is a lousy teacher. It seduces smart people into thinking they can't lose." I also went to sites where I could download replays to learn how the top players play (this was before YouTube and Twitch).

The more knowledge I gain, the more ideas I come up with. The bottom line is that learning leads to new ideas and gives you new perspectives on life. New ideas spark new action plans. And those actions lead to achievements. Burn this into your brain: the more knowledge you acquire, the more ideas you can execute. And although many of your ideas will fail, your successes will more than make up for your failures.

Never Peak

I caught up recently with David Hua, who runs Meadow, a cannabis delivery startup. I used to intern for David when I was in college at a company he cofounded called GotGame. It was basically Twitch before its time.

I asked him what his biggest lesson was when it came to learning and he said, "Never peak": "There is always something new to learn and always room for improvement. I often learn the best from doing, but the execution is also shaped by listening to those who have shared their experience. With continuous learning, you have an endless mountain to climb and the joy of helping others along in the summit."

The reality
of life is that it's
**an exercise
in always
learning more.**

Because you have reached level 4 in the book, you get a new feature added to each chapter moving forward: insights from *Leveling Up* podcast guests.

From the *Leveling Up* Podcast: Emerson Spartz

Emerson Spartz is the founder of Spartz Media and a *New York Times*–bestselling author. He dropped out of *middle school* and has built many online properties, which collectively earn over 160 million monthly page views.

At twelve years old, Emerson convinced his parents to let him drop out of school and homeschool himself. Meanwhile, his site MuggleNet.com grew to fifty million page views a month, forcing Emerson to grow up quickly. MuggleNet.com wasn't just a stand-alone website. It was a collection of different properties from online forums, fan sites, and books. Emerson also had the number-one podcast—not just about Harry Potter but the top podcast in the *world*.

While most people consider virality to be the hard part, for Emerson managing people has been the most difficult. At age twelve, he was managing a team of 120 employees and volunteers. He kept his age a secret, knowing people wouldn't be interested working with a kid. Eventually he came clean and people weren't surprised. Today Emerson has been managing people over half of his life.

Emerson's unique and highly profitable self-education taught him how to code, write, edit, lead, manage, and design. His parents (smartly) stayed out of his way and let him take an unschooling approach to his education. But one thing they did request was that Emerson read four short biographies of successful people every day. Emerson said, "This just shattered my twelve-year-old brain into about 10,000 pieces and I started to think really big."

From reading the biographies, Emerson quickly realized that people who change the world are extraordinarily influential *before* they change the world. He realized influence and impact were closely linked. The more influence you have, the more impact you can make. Emerson also wondered if he could do all of these things at age twelve, what could he do at seventeen? Instead of stopping with MuggleNet.com, he decided to think big and change the world.

Emerson figured if he could make things go viral, that would be the closest you could get to having an immense superpower. He sees the power of virality as a tool to spread powerful messages to help causes for good around the world.

You can listen to my interview with Emerson Spartz by searching "Leveling Up Emerson Spartz" or by going to LevelingUp.com/growth-everywhere-interview/emerson-spartz.

GAMIFY YOUR LIFE
WITH THESE POWER TIPS

Growth is one of the most important power-ups to harness in life. It leads to more challenging opportunities as you play the game of life. Someone who does not grow does not get to level up into more challenging stages. Only the growth-minded get to the best opportunities.

- You can download and listen to most podcasts for free. For ios, use the Podcasts app or Overcast (my preferred app). For Android, use the Google Play or Stitcher app. Spotify, Pandora, SoundCloud, and YouTube are also options.

- I host two podcasts. *Marketing School*, which I cohost with Neil Patel, teaches people the ins and outs of marketing for five to ten minutes a day. We've gotten emails from people saying they have gotten jobs without degrees thanks to what they've learned by listening to the podcast. Other people have said they went from having no revenue to up to $75,000 in revenue just by implementing some of the changes they've learned. On *Leveling Up*, I interview world-class entrepreneurs who have founded companies that have sold for millions (or even billions). We talk about marketing, entrepreneurship, and productivity.

- As you get better at listening to audio content, try switching the speed to 1.5× or 2×. You'll be increasing your rate of learning. Yes, your retention might drop, but the ultimate goal is to get at least one good idea from whatever you consume. Don't try to bite off more than you can chew.

- You can use services like Blinkist to get book summaries. If you like the summary, you can read the whole book.

- Sites like YouTube, Skillshare, Udacity, Udemy, Khan Academy, and Coursera are all great for learning subjects online.

- Use mobile apps such as Feedly to save your favorite blogs. Then combine it with Pocket to save online reading material for later. Pocket integrates with many other tools and is great for transferring your readings to desktop, mobile, or tablet. It can also read the article to you if you prefer audio.

- Twitter can be invaluable if you learn how to harness its power by tuning out the noise. Follow only the people who you respect the most and put them into a "list." That will allow you to tune out most of the negativity and general noise.

- Be very careful about your information diet. If you are taking in negativity and crisis, your mind will not be in a good space to solve problems. Reduce your media intake, and focus on information from people who will help you grow.

Be very careful about your information diet. **Focus on information from people who will help you grow.**

QUEST: DIVE DEEP

△ **YOUR POWER-UP** △
A new treasure of knowledge—
and a map to finding more

× **QUEST DEADLINE** ×
7 days

PLEASE FINISH THE quest before moving on to the next level!

1 What topics are you interested in right now? Which of these topics do you think are important to our world? Home in on the topic that you think can make the greatest impact on the world. Something you're truly passionate about; something you can get behind.

2 Do a deep dive into the topic. Make lists of:

A The top ten blogs related to your topic.
B The top ten books on your topic.
C The top ten people to talk to about the topic.

3 Create an action plan for learning as much as you can in a few days—for example:

A Day 1: Spend at least one hour a day reading the best blog posts on the topic.

B Day 2: Pick a book and read it for at least one hour a day until you finish the book.

C Day 3: Start talking to people—go to where these people are hanging out. Some might be on a subreddit on Reddit.

Or in a Facebook group. Or in a Slack or Discord group. Or Quora. Or Twitter. Do some digging and find where these communities are and join a few. Then start engaging people with your questions.

D Day 4: By now, you should have identified researcher names that continually pop up in the topic area. Try to reach out to at least ten of them and ask a burning question you have on your mind. At least one should reach out to you after a few attempts. (Don't give up if they don't respond on the first attempt.)

See what results you can accomplish and how you feel after doing the work. And remember that, as Cheri Huber said, "How you do anything is how you do everything."

Congratulations!
You just got a bonus.

You acquired the **G** power-up from the **GAMER** framework. Acquire all of these power-ups from the book to unlock the framework to help you grow forever.

Go to **LevelingUp.com/g** and enter in password "**G**" to get your power-up bonus.

ROUTINES

NEW! Level 5
acquired!

In progress

"I hated every minute
of training, but I said,
'Don't quit. Suffer now
and live the rest of your
life as a champion.'"

MUHAMMAD ALI

THINK ABOUT YOUR HEROES. Are they athletes, Nobel Prize winners, champion gamers, or close family members? Why are these people your heroes?

In elementary school, I always played games like *Diablo* and *Warcraft* as late as my parents would allow: ten p.m.

In middle school and high school, I played games like *StarCraft*, *Quake*, *Counter-Strike*, and *EverQuest* as late as my parents allowed me to (a slight upgrade): midnight.

In college, I ramped it up. I stayed up until between three and six a.m. playing games: *World of Warcraft*, *Warcraft III*, *Defense of the Ancients*, and poker. I reached the pinnacle in some of these games not because of my talent or intellect.

It was because of my habits.

Apple CEO Tim Cook is at the gym by five a.m. before his day gets crazy.

Quest Nutrition's cofounder Tom Bilyeu is up between 3:30 and four a.m. to get a head start on the day.

When I spoke with billionaire Naveen Jain on the *Leveling Up* podcast, he nonchalantly said that he wakes up at 4:30 a.m. to read for two hours. When I asked him why, he said he's excited to wake up to work on his projects because they're fun.

NBA legend Kobe Bryant was known for his exceptional work ethic. On YouTube, you'll find video of him shooting until 3:30 in the morning after a loss to the Miami Heat. He was also known for waking up at unreal hours to practice his jump shots. Even legendary NBA coach Phil Jackson, who coached Kobe Bryant and Michael Jordan, said Bryant's work ethic was superior to Jordan's. That's saying a lot when you're comparing someone to the greatest basketball player of all time.

Before I go further, I want to make it clear that working extra hours doesn't necessarily equate to success. In fact, overexertion can lead to poor long-term performance. That being said, hard work typically pays off, and it's a delicate balance that only you can find in your life.

The Michael Jordan of Gaming

I caught up with Dennis Fong, aka Thresh, on this topic. Dennis is known as the world's first pro gamer, or "the Michael Jordan of gaming," according to the *Wall Street Journal*. In the late '90s when gaming started to take off, Dennis became a top player in the first-person shooter game *Quake*. He won tournaments that awarded him cash prizes and even Ferraris. He was sponsored by companies like Microsoft. He became a true eSports pro before eSports was a thing.

Dennis always knew he wanted to take his competitiveness into the next arena, which he decided was business. In 1996, he used his endorsements to start his first company, Gamers.com. He then went on to start numerous other businesses. He said his gaming experiences taught him to anticipate things before others did, and that allowed him to pick his business ventures without much effort.

Dennis's habits allowed him to seamlessly transition from a pro gamer into a serial entrepreneur. And even after seeing success, he still continues to work hard. He told me some of his key habits are waking up early to work on important things and staying in shape.

Each level of life requires you to add something to propel you to the next step. Identifying and consistently practicing appropriate habits is a challenge, but if done well, it can accelerate your pace of leveling up.

That's the power of tiny gains, as explained by James Clear in *Atomic Habits*: "improving by 1 percent isn't particularly notable—sometimes it isn't even *noticeable*—but it can be far more meaningful, especially in the long run."

THE POWER OF TINY GAINS

1% better every day $1.01^{365} =$ **37.78**
1% worse every day $0.99^{365} =$ **0.03**

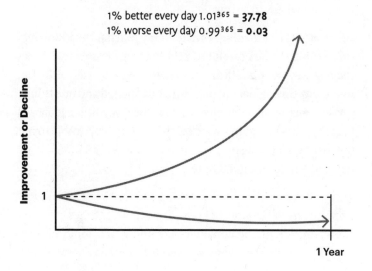

My Habit Journal

To provide inspiration, here's a list of habits that I check off on my phone every day at nine p.m. It's like a habit journal.

- **Wake up by six a.m.** Although I'm usually awake before 5:30, this habit forces me to be out of bed by six so I can get my day started. Six to nine a.m. is usually my time when nobody can disrupt me. I use this time to accomplish one big task before the craziness of the day hits.

- **Recite goals.** Every December, I set my goals for the new year and I try to focus on a few key things. I recite these goals and the related key steps every morning. For example, let's say I want my podcast to reach 2.5 million downloads per month by the end of the year. I'll say that and then talk about the one or two key things I need to do to get there. That way I have direction when I start my day.

- **Journal.** Every morning, I write in my journal the following: three things to be grateful for, three things that would make today great, and one affirmation. Before I go to bed, I write the following: three amazing things that happened and one thing I can improve upon. (Search online for the Five Minute Journal.) I used to view journaling as excessive and not applicable to me, but after giving it a shot, I realized it can set the tone for my day and end it on a good note.

- **Train.** This could be called "working out," but I call it "training" because one of the world's greatest strength coaches says that exercising should be considered training. It's about improving, rather than struggling to exercise every day because you "should." Remember it's all about how things are framed.

Each level
of life requires
you to add
**something to
propel you to
the next step.**

- **Accomplish one big thing.** Every single day is an opportunity to do something amazing. If I can do one big thing that moves the needle in the right direction, I know I'm going to be satisfied with the day. Remember time is the only resource that cannot be renewed. Make the most of it.

- **Goof off for at least thirty minutes.** Even though I find my work very enjoyable (being able to work on whatever I want to work on daily is awesome), I still want to dedicate time to goof around. Typically, that's watching funny videos or TV shows.

- **Sleep for eight hours.** When I used to sleep for five to six hours, I thought I deserved a badge of honor. But the reality is for me (and for most humans), I need eight hours to function at a high level. With five to six hours of sleep, I'm only able to perform at a fraction of my capacity.

Now keep in mind that you don't need to take on all of these habits. I have included practical tips on how to get started with habit creation toward the end of this chapter.

From the *Leveling Up* Podcast: Noah Kagan

Noah Kagan has a list of accomplishments: the thirtieth employee at Facebook, fifth at Mint, and founder of multiple multi-million-dollar companies, including AppSumo. He's built a personal brand around entrepreneurship, and I was fortunate enough to interview him twice over a five-year period.

What is the secret to his success? What are his habits?

First, he's very transparent about his successes and failures. Although he was the thirtieth employee at Facebook, he was fired and lost out on what would have been a $100 million payout. Ouch. The related habit he cultivated was reflection. In this case, he learned that making mistakes in life is perfectly fine, but not learning from those mistakes can be fatal.

Noah is also very numbers-driven and sets clear goals for his companies to hit. And when his companies don't hit their goals, his teams go through the habit of reflecting on what went wrong and then adjusting accordingly. Just like he does.

Noah decided to cultivate fitness and healthy diet habits, because they contribute directly to him being more effective in his day-to-day activities.

Is Noah some kind of superhuman? No. We all have our bad habits and indulgences. (Noah's happens to be tacos.) But if you build a good habit system, then you'll be on your way to achieving your dreams.

You can listen to my interview with Noah Kagan by searching "Leveling Up Noah Kagan" or by going to LevelingUp.com/growth-everywhere-interview/noah-kagan-appsumo.

GAMIFY YOUR LIFE WITH THESE POWER TIPS

- Use a notebook, spreadsheet, or an app like Way of Life to track the progress on your daily habits. For example, if you want to start flossing more, sleeping longer, or waking up earlier, you can easily input those into the app and check off whatever you complete. Completing habits consecutively allows you to form a streak, so you'll be motivated to keep it going. It's a nice way of gamifying your life!

- Search on Google and YouTube for "tiny habits" and learn how to implement small habits. It's tough to start a new habit from scratch. Tiny habits allow you to gradually warm up to your new habits.

- Write down your goals on Post-its and put them where you'll see them daily. I have Post-its on my bathroom mirror and on the edge of my computer screen so they're constantly front of mind.

- James Clear, who wrote the fantastic book *Atomic Habits*, was on the *Leveling Up* podcast, so give it a listen when you get a chance. He has a great newsletter on habits as well—and it's free.

- Use the Eisenhower box to help prioritize your daily tasks. Your most important boxes are Urgent/Important and Not Urgent/Important. You might think Urgent/Important is the box to focus on, but Not Urgent/Important is often crucial because its tasks usually revolve around longer-term thinking. For the other boxes, figure out how to delegate or ignore those tasks altogether. Using the Eisenhower box will help you prioritize and focus on what's most important.

THE EISENHOWER BOX

	URGENT	NOT URGENT
IMPORTANT	**DO** *Do it now.* • Write article for today	**DECIDE** *Schedule a time to do it.* • Exercising • Calling family and friends • Researching articles • Long-term biz strategy
NOT IMPORTANT	**DELEGATE** *Who can do it for you?* • Scheduling interviews • Booking flights • Approving comments • Answering certain emails • Sharing articles	**DELETE** *Eliminate it.* • Watching TV • Checking social media • Sorting through junk mail

QUEST: MANAGE YOUR HABITS

Advanced consciousness and better
control of your actions

✕ **QUEST DEADLINE** ✕
7 days

PLEASE CONTINUE READING as you do this quest!

1   List your daily habits in one of two columns: positive habits
and negative habits. We all have positive and negative habits, so it's okay to be honest with yourself. The key is getting
started with good habits while reducing bad habits.

A   Positive habits might be writing in your journal every morning, meditating, eating healthy, or getting enough sleep.
B   Negative habits might be watching too much TV, smoking,
etc.

2   After you complete this chart, focus on:

A   One negative habit that you would like to cut down on and
eventually eliminate altogether. First focus on a week-long
period, then a thirty-day period. For example, if you eat fast
food every day, cut it to three times the first week, then continue to reduce it further for a month.

B One positive habit you would like to double down on. For example, if you're writing 500 words a day, try to double it to 1,000 words a day and see how you feel after a week. Then make a plan for the next month.

Your first quest is the first week. You need to complete the trial reduction of the bad habit and the trial increase of the good habit for seven days before you can level up. Then your ongoing quest, continuing after you move on to the next level, is the next month . . . and then onward from that.

You'll start to stack habits over the course of your life as different things become more important to you. You'll also drop habits that lose importance. So don't sweat it if you don't have the "perfect" set of habits. It's a constant work in progress.

LEVEL
6

APPRENTICE MENTALITY

NEW! Level 6
acquired!

In progress

"In the beginner's mind there are many possibilities, but in the expert's there are few."

SHUNRYU SUZUKI

REMEMBER I TALKED about the "newbie mindset" in level 1? It's tough to maintain that mindset as you advance in your life. As you get stronger, you don't want to lose the freshness of being a newbie. This chapter will help reinforce your freshness.

When I first started to play *Defense of the Ancients* (it's similar to *League of Legends*), the game was brand new and there were no popular strategies or tactics on how to play. I dominated the game because it was the wild, wild west. Then I didn't touch the game for a year or so, during which time my friends started playing. Being the cocky kid I was, I thought I could waltz back in and establish the same level of dominance I once had.

I got my butt handed to me by my friends. Over and over. It was embarrassing.

I tried to bulldoze my way into becoming better because I thought I deserved to be handed back my "rightful" place of top player. Instead of learning by watching game footage and analyzing my mistakes, I let my ego get the best of me and I never returned to my previous form.

Great gamers and athletes alike spend countless hours honing their craft so they can improve on all the little nuances that add up to make them elite players. They also often maintain a beginner's mindset.

Think about a time when you started to learn something completely foreign, such as a new language or skill. Your mind was completely open and willing to accept any lessons that came your way, right? That's the apprentice mentality.

When you become skilled at something, you tend to close yourself off to other ideas because you now have rules about how things work based on your experience. That's human nature: to defend and protect what we become used to.

For example, Kodak was a multi-billion-dollar company that saw the advent of digital photography bring it to bankruptcy. Although Kodak owned the patents to digital photography, they dismissed it as a fad and continued to focus on dying technologies. Eventually, digital photography became the new norm. By the time Kodak noticed, it was too late. This is known as "disruption" in the technology world. When incumbents in the space aren't paying attention or adapting, they risk being devoured.

In contrast, Google started out as a search engine and has since branched out into areas such as self-driving cars, in-home accessories, mobile phones, and more. Its parent company, Alphabet, also invested billions into artificial intelligence because it predicts that AI will make a monumental shift in our near future.

Another one of Alphabet's moonshots is trying to solve death. Now *that's* having a beginner's mind.

When I interviewed Moon Express founder Naveen Jain on the *Leveling Up* podcast, I found he had a knack for taking moonshots, too. What else could explain his desire to make illnesses "optional" or fly to the moon?

Despite being a billionaire and having zero need to ever work again, Naveen enjoys learning new things and then executing on that knowledge to make a difference in the world. When I asked him what the difference is between billionaires and millionaires, his answer was simple: billionaires think bigger than millionaires. And the secret to consistently thinking bigger? Learning as much as you can to keep yourself hungry for more.

Don't Stop Beginning

As a gamer, I often found myself playing close to an elite level: winning online poker tournaments with thousands of players; being part of top guilds in *World of Warcraft*, *EverQuest*, *Warcraft III*, and more. I always wanted to be among the best because it gave me a sense of accomplishment.

However, whenever I started to excel, I became complacent. I was invited to join a top-rated *Counter-Strike* team when I was in high school. During tryouts, I stood far and away above the rest of the players with a record of thirty-three kills to one death. The team put me on a two-week trial during which I could play in scrimmages with other top *Counter-Strike* teams. The deal was if they liked me after the evaluation period, they would promote me from a recruit to a full-time member. I thought I had made it.

Then it was time to play our first scrimmage against a rival clan. I didn't practice at all and barely communicated with the team beforehand. When the first scrimmage started, I became a liability. I ended with a poor ratio of three kills to twelve deaths. The poor results continued during subsequent matches, and I made *zero* adjustments in those weeks. This eventually led to me getting kicked off the team.

The more power-up stacking you do, **the more of an advantage you'll have in business and in life.**

For weeks, I couldn't understand what happened. Then I realized: I thought I was way better than I really was. I thought I was an expert. And experts don't need to practice, right?

Wrong.

That's the problem with being too rooted in the expert's mindset. Experts can't get out of their own head. As I look back on my gaming history, I see a trend. When I started to play at a high level, I not only became arrogant in my style of play, but I became short-tempered with my teammates (whom I saw as my siblings), my friends, and my family.

When I was growing up, I thought the experts—also known as the adults—had it figured out. They always had all the answers due to their experiences and that's why I looked up to them. But as I got older, I realized the standouts in life and business were the ones who were constantly reinventing themselves—and didn't always know the answers.

Refresh Your Mind

The late Steve Jobs dropped out of Reed College after one semester, backpacked in India, and took psychedelic drugs. Those experiences helped him cocreate one of the world's most valuable brands in Apple. I'm not saying you need to quit school, travel to a foreign country, or take drugs. I'm just pointing out how Steve Jobs knew that school wasn't right for him, so he started with a fresh mindset by going on his journey.

After Apple became a public company, it went through a period of struggle that eventually saw Jobs ousted from the company. Apple went on to suffer through the next few years before Mr. Jobs was finally reinstated to lead the company back to its glory. When Jobs came back, he said he'd had a lot of time to reflect and came back as a different person. That period of reflection allowed him to start the mobile revolution, which led to the iPhone, iPad, and a completely refreshed product line. This catapulted Apple into becoming the most valuable company in the world.

It might be simple to start with a newbie's mindset, but it can be difficult to retain it once you achieve some level of success. We see this in the story of Steve Jobs and it can also be seen in my own gaming history.

Your habits make you who you are. And having a beginner's mindset can help you cultivate great habits to set you up for long-term success. Notice the chaining of two power-ups together—good habits and the apprentice mentality. The more power-up stacking you do, the more of an advantage you'll have in business and in life.

Add humility as yet another related power-up. Understanding that there is always someone smarter than you allows you to open your mind to bigger and better opportunities. Closed mindsets only offer you the chance to play in the world you already understand. The newbie's mindset is an essential power-up in life gamification because it opens the door for growth.

From the *Leveling Up* Podcast: Andy Mackensen and Sean Kelly

I was fortunate enough to interview two cofounders I interned for a long time ago, Andy Mackensen and Sean Kelly. When I interned for them, their business focused on distributing healthy vending machines, and they were doing $0 in revenue. In a short time, they shot past $25 million in annual revenue.

However, they soon realized that healthy vending machines were not their true calling. They changed their business model to providing healthy office snacks. That led to healthy snack delivery to offices that wanted to better options for their employees.

Their new business, SnackNation, is now on fire. They wouldn't have been able to evolve if they both weren't hungry to continually try new things with a beginner's mindset. It's hard to move from a successful business model (vending machines) to a new one (office snacks) and then shift it into something new (healthy snack delivery). But a beginner's mindset allows you to explore possibilities without being chained down by your past experiences.

▬▬▬

You can listen to my interviews with the two founders by searching "Leveling Up Andy Mackensen" and "Leveling Up Sean Kelly" or by going to LevelingUp.com/growth-everywhere-interview/andymackensen and LevelingUp.com/growth-everywhere-interview/sean-kelly-snacknation.

GAMIFY YOUR LIFE WITH THESE POWER TIPS

- Listen to the audiobook of *Zen Mind, Beginner's Mind* by Shunryu Suzuki. Allow yourself to spend as long as you need to fully comprehend what it means to have a beginner's mind.

- Backtrack to the last time you were arrogant about a situation or thought you were "too good" to learn something new. Is there something you could have improved on? What could you have done better? Were you truly "too good" or were you holding yourself back?

- In order to truly improve, you must unlearn old habits and continue to evolve. For example, you might've learned in school that a report should be three to four pages long. However, the internet world might prefer something far shorter. Have a strong opinion, but be willing to listen and adapt.

- Today, there are countless ways to start as a beginner. Khan Academy can get you started on the basics of many subjects, such as computer science. YouTube has many creators making incredible free educational content. My cousin learned how to build out his garden just from watching YouTube videos. Take advantage of it! Codecademy is a free online coding school. *Marketing School*, my podcast, provides free daily tips on marketing and more.

A newbie's mindset allows you to explore possibilities **without being chained down by your past experiences.**

QUEST: REFRESH YOUR BEGINNER'S MIND

△ **YOUR POWER-UP** △
A fresh brain

✕ **QUEST DEADLINE** ✕
2 hours

CHARLIE MUNGER, ONE of the world's greatest investors, often talks about being able to articulate the opposition's argument better than they can. That means being able to look at all points of view when broaching a topic. Your quest is to practice doing this yourself.

1 Think of something in the world today that you are highly opposed to.

2 Assign yourself to prepare a debate *in favor* of it.

3 Take the time to research it.

A Think of all the objections you would normally raise.

B Find answers to them that actually make sense from a rational perspective.

4 See if you can formulate a better argument in favor of it than its advocates have.

A Work out the best possible arguments *against* your own usual position.

B I don't need to tell you to formulate your own arguments in response to those arguments. You won't be able to keep yourself from doing that. Just make sure you assume nothing. And then see how well you can counter those arguments in turn.

Doing this exercise will help your mind open up to the different possibilities around you. And an open mind is a core quality of a newbie's mindset.

LEVEL 7

GRIT

NEW! Level 7
acquired!

In progress

"If you're going through hell, keep going."

WINSTON CHURCHILL

GROWING UP, we were taught to strive to get straight As in school. And if we were privileged enough, our parents might have spent money to send us to after-school tutoring to give us an edge.

I grew up thinking the kids who got straight As were geniuses. But I never really cared for school—nor did I understand the purpose of being forced to sit down and spend my time in classes I didn't care about.

I didn't care about history. I didn't care about math. I didn't care about physical education (the pungent locker-room body odor brought me close to throwing up on countless occasions). I didn't care about any of these subjects because they weren't relevant to my interests. And so my grades were subpar in high school and I was almost kicked out for nearly flunking a required class in my senior year. That's right. Almost kicked out—of *high school*!

As I mentioned before, I was then almost kicked out of college for missing too many classes and failing tests. I remember looking at my report card after the first year and seeing six withdraws and a few Fs. I faked my report cards to keep my parents at bay, and inside I was a complete mess. I knew I would have to somehow claw my way back and eventually transfer to a different college if I wanted to graduate with a meaningful degree. I got accepted as a transfer student to the University of California, San Diego (UCSD)—and then my acceptance got rescinded because my grades regressed again.

I felt hopeless and I didn't want to let my parents down after all the money they had invested in me and my college tuition, so I decided to fight. I first drove down from Los Angeles to San Diego to plead my case with a UCSD chancellor. This is roughly a six-hour round trip in traffic. The first time I made the trip, I was quickly waved off and told there was no chance.

I drove down a second time. Same result.

I even wrote a two-page appeal letter!

On the third trip, I was finally able to break through and the chancellor decided to give me a shot. Probably so I would stop bothering her.

The upshot is that I failed my way through my school years and barely made it out because following a straight path didn't feel right to me. School never made logical sense to me because the premise was built on following the rules of a system. I was never built for following rules—I always wanted to do my own thing.

Can You Hack the Route to Success?

Although I don't think being an entrepreneur is in everyone's blood, I think everyone aspires to be entrepreneurial. *Everyone* dreams of having something they can call their own. And those dreams are never really linear.

Most people think the path to success is a straight line up. The reality is that success, however you define it, is a journey

SUCCESS   **SUCCESS**

What people think   What it really
it looks like.   looks like.

filled with turbulence and lots of ups and downs. That makes
sense, right? And the important thing to realize is that the
difference between successful people and average people is
simply their willingness to ride the rough winds and persevere.

In my life experiences, and from what I've seen by studying
other successful people, the path to success is overwhelmingly
exponential. That is, individuals keep getting punched in the
face over and over for years—and then eventually things take off.

Think of a hockey-stick-shaped graph like the one on the
next page.

The nearly straight line is years of slogging away with
almost no results. The upward curve is when the "overnight
success" happens. What most people don't see is the amount
of work it took to achieve that "overnight success."

When I think of success, I think of a particular quotation
from Winston Churchill: "Success is the ability to move from
one failure to another without loss of enthusiasm." For me,

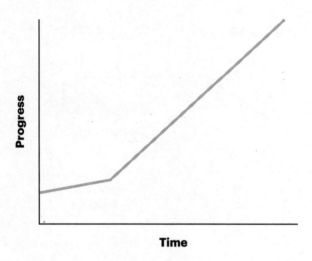

that represents gaming in a nutshell. Putting in the hard work was a simple matter of paying my dues. I understood the growing pains I'd have to go through in each game to get good.

This lesson had never been taught to me because I never did spectacularly well in school nor was I ever on a sports team. I hadn't bought in to either of those goals. The difference for me was that because I enjoyed what I did as a gamer, I didn't consider the pain I was going through to be a game-stopper.

Most people don't know that I was able to buy my ad agency, Single Grain, for $2 out of pocket. Those who do probably consider that to be a major success—but it wasn't in the beginning. In my first year, I attempted to pivot the business from an SEO services company to a content marketing services company.

I made countless cringeworthy mistakes such as reading a book called *Let My People Go Surfing* and then taking its title literally by not showing up to the office and letting employees do whatever they wanted to do. At one point, one of the team members called me and said there were people in the office watching *Family Guy* all day and eating chips. This is not to blame the book—the book was incredible—I was just an idiot!

I came very close to quitting and even verbally agreed to take a full-time job in Dallas, Texas. Fortunately, Single Grain saw some semblance of traction with its paid advertising service, and we decided to put all of our efforts into that. From there, the company was able to grow predictably and still continues to today.

A key takeaway from the Single Grain experience for me was the necessity of being able to tread water for as long as possible. My podcast cohost, Neil, and I always talk about how it seems that three years is usually what it takes for something to be successful.

If you're aiming to achieve something, be prepared to go through pain. How much pain you're willing to endure is an indicator of how far you will go.

The hack: do something that you enjoy so you feel less pain.

The Struggle Is the Game

Many people talk about doing something they love. But, in truth, that doesn't mean they are not struggling. It's that the psychological effect of their struggles is dampened by them having fun.

Let's think about the progression of an elite gamer:

- Start out as a newbie and get crushed by your competition over and over.

Success is a journey filled with turbulence.

- Learn from your mistakes and start to improve.
- Watch replays from experts to level up your skills.
- Start to stream your videos on sites like Twitch and YouTube.
- Join a team of people with complementary skill sets.
- Continue to improve until you're at an elite level.
- Join a world-class team and compete for championships.

You're *always* going to struggle through moments when you're on the path to greatness. That's just the price you must pay.

Walt Disney was rejected over 200 times on his proposal for Disneyland. In fact, he and his brother failed for ten years before they started to gain traction. Former Starbucks CEO Howard Schultz was declined by 242 banks when he tried to inject money into his coffee business. Now-billionaire Oprah Winfrey was classified as "unfit for TV" and was fired from multiple jobs. Movie director Steven Spielberg didn't get into the University of Southern California's film school the three times he applied.

One of the most remarkable examples of grit is the perseverance of American football quarterback Tom Brady. When he played in college, he was not even the starter on his team. In his draft year, he was picked in the seventh round (which typically means scouts did not view him in high regard and he was likely to be cut). Scouts said in his pre-draft evaluation videos that they saw limited athleticism, an average throwing arm, and just an all-around mediocre player.

When Brady first reported to practice, he looked the owner dead in the eye and told him he was the "best decision" the team had ever made. Brady went on to win the most championship rings of any quarterback in NFL history.

Brady had everything going against him, and throughout his career he has faced criticism. But never once did he let that affect his results. That's how he came to be known as "the greatest of all time," or the GOAT, of the National Football League.

In his seventh Super Bowl, Brady's team was down by twenty-five points. No NFL team had ever come back from twenty-five down to win it. Tom Brady pulled it off by telling his teammates to take the rest of the game one play at a time—to power his team through adversity to win his fifth championship ring. To be able to not give up after facing seemingly insurmountable odds on the biggest stage is a prime example of grit—and that's what it takes to win a championship. As of this writing, Tom Brady has now played in nine Super Bowls and won six of them (the most of any quarterback in American football history).

The Best Fuel

What do these stories tell you? That greatness takes persistence. And what fuels that persistence?

Sometimes I wonder what got me to where I am right now. I'm by no means a billionaire, athlete, or movie star, but being able to wake up every morning to work on what I want to work on and cause change in others is incredibly fulfilling.

This is probably why I get along so well with my podcast cohost and good friend, Neil Patel. He's a *New York Times*–bestselling author and was recognized by the United Nations and President Obama as a top 100 entrepreneur under the age of thirty-five. He has founded multiple software and service-based companies. And we both wake up every morning excited to talk about what we're working on. Being passionate helps foster persistence.

Angela Duckworth, author of *Grit: The Power of Passion and Perseverance*, said, "I won't just have a job; I'll have a calling. I'll challenge myself every day. When I get knocked down, I'll get back up. I may not be the smartest person in the room, but I'll strive to be the grittiest."

Because I'm passionate about learning and teaching others, it helps me push through the inevitable adversity I'll face along the way. Without passion, it's hard to find the energy to fight through challenges.

The right quest combined with grit is a virtually unstoppable combination to reach the success that you desire. Remember that part of success is how much pain tolerance you have. The more you can take, the likelier you are to win.

Whenever you think about the tough times you're going through, just remember one thing: tough times don't last; tough people do!

From the *Leveling Up* Podcast: Ron Klein

Ron Klein is the inventor of the magnetic credit card stripe (the stripe you see on the back of credit cards) and is known as the "Grandfather of Possibilities." His inventions have affected billions of people around the world. Even now, in his eighties, he continues to work on new innovations for budding entrepreneurs and, in particular, blind people.

When Ron was sixteen, he mysteriously contracted a hepatitis infection and, after three months in the hospital, convalesced at home—for a year and a half. He couldn't go to school or do much of anything, but he decided to take the situation as an opportunity and a challenge. In a year and a half, he read eighteen volumes of the *Encyclopaedia Britannica* cover to cover.

Ron later suffered an injury from his military service and multiple car accidents that left him with a serious spine condition. Even today, he still can't stand for long or walk far. To him, this was just another challenge. He read *Gray's Anatomy* cover to cover while riding on a stationary bicycle to stay in shape. Eventually, he started participating in triathlons and won gold medals with his team. He eyed the Olympics and was recognized as Florida's athlete of the year in his sixties. He ended up winning gold in the Senior Games. He still bikes thirty miles every day to help control and relieve his pain.

If you need motivation to persevere, Ron Klein's story is the perfect listen for you.

You can listen to my interview with Ron Klein by searching "Leveling Up Ron Klein" or by going to LevelingUp.com/growth-everywhere-interview/ron-klein.

GAMIFY YOUR LIFE WITH THESE POWER TIPS

As you have seen in this chapter, any individual who has achieved success has had to persevere. It is the toll that must be paid. So how do you do this? Try leveling up with these Power Tips.

- Next time you find yourself wanting to give up or "take it easy" during a stressful moment (such as working out or a mentally taxing task), see if you can kick it into overdrive and push extra hard. Try it another few times and see how you feel afterward!

- Watch Angela Duckworth's short TED Talk "Grit: The Power of Passion and Perseverance," available on YouTube.

QUEST: GIVE IT A SHOT

PLEASE CONTINUE READING as you go through the quest!

1. Identify one thing that you secretly want to do but fear always gets in the way of you doing it.

2. Work out the steps to achieving it. What's the first thing you need to overcome to do it? What's the next? And so on.

3. For each step, list the worst and best outcomes.

4. Note the benefits of taking each action. Then note the consequences of not taking that action in a six-month period, a twelve-month period, and a thirty-six-month period. These will be the consequences if you choose not to break through barriers to take your desired actions.

5. Then go out and break through the first barrier.

That's your starting quest. Your ongoing quest is to break through each barrier one by one. It's not a ten-ton dragon—it's ten tons of not-too-large lizards, coming one at a time.

Make a list of three things you want to try this month and genuinely give each a shot. Try *at least* one thing.

Record in a spreadsheet the quests you want to try, when you start them, when they end, and what the result was. If you're not measuring your success, you're not managing it. This is known as feedback analysis.

8

ALCHEMY

NEW! Level 8
acquired!

In progress

"I have always said that everyone is in sales. Maybe you don't hold the title of salesperson, but if the business you are in requires you to deal with people, you, my friend, are in sales."

ZIG ZIGLAR

ALCHEMY IS AN apparently magical process of transformation, creation, or combination. In many of the games I played where magic and sorcery were involved, an alchemist could create gold coins out of thin air.

The cool thing is that this can actually be done in real life—well, at least the part about creating money from nowhere. The two skills that combine together to create alchemy are marketing and sales.

I know, I know, it feels a little scary, even slimy, but I promise you that it's not.

Most people talk about how much they "hate" sales and marketing. I hear people say all the time that they're "not salespeople." That bothers me because the reality is *everyone* is marketing and selling themselves all the time. The first impression you give on a job interview. The first impression you give on a date. The first impression you make with a potential client. The list goes on.

Everything you own and everything around you has been marketed and sold. Glasses. Phones. Computers. Pencils. Toilet paper. *Everything.*

Obama and Trump had one thing in common: a strong promise for Americans. Obama's was "Hope"; Trump's was "Make America Great Again." Their opponents did not have a message that could beat theirs. Obama and Trump emerged victorious in part due to strong marketing and messaging. I'm not being political here: I appreciate good marketing when I see it.

During my early gaming days, one of the most important goals I set for every team-based game was to make it onto a high-end team. I knew this was 100 percent necessary to accomplish the things that only the best could do.

If I wanted the best weapons and armor in *World of Warcraft* or *EverQuest*, I had to be able to defeat the hardest bosses in a game, which meant I had to join the best guild. If I wanted to compete against only the best *Counter-Strike* clans to win championships, I had to play with the best.

But pay attention to my previous two sentences: I just talked about myself and what "I" wanted. As it turns out, being selfish is a fatal mistake most people make.

Give to Get

Back in the day, I pestered people and tried to brute-force my way into getting what I wanted. As a result, I was often ignored because I kept begging for something without providing any value to the other party.

What I eventually learned was that providing value to people *before* asking for anything was the best way to get my foot in the door. It's the same with any relationship in real life: give before taking. Always think about what's in it for *them* before you think about yourself.

After I learned that, I reached out to individuals on top teams in order to build relationships with them. They would then invite me to small group dungeon raids or public matches where the stakes weren't high. Once I'd built up enough trust, I'd get invited to large dragon raids and scrimmages where the rest of the team would evaluate if I was a good fit or not. This strategy of giving first before taking was a lightbulb moment for me and has stayed with me ever since.

One of my businesses, Single Grain, is a marketing agency that helps brands such as Amazon, Salesforce, Nordstrom, Uber, and more. Our business is predicated on bringing people to the point of sale through marketing. Here are some examples of our own marketing:

- **Podcasts.** We have two podcasts we host where we talk about entrepreneurship and marketing. These podcasts cover ground on entrepreneurs who are looking to grow their businesses or people looking to learn marketing (who can then join our team!). Podcasts are great because they hold the attention of the listener while they are cleaning, working out, or doing another task. *Marketing School*, my daily marketing podcast, gets about one million downloads per month. *Leveling Up*, my weekly entrepreneurial podcast, gets about 100,000 downloads per month. All because we stuck with the goal of providing people with value.

- **Blog.** We create lots of written educational content on our blog to teach people about the new things that are going on in the marketing industry. This helps us build SEO traffic from Google and also makes us an authority in the space.

- **Videos.** In addition to this book, we have a video series called *Leveling Up* where we go into businesses and learn their stories, see what their challenges are, and teach marketing lessons.

- **Events.** From dinners to conferences, we host our own events to better connect with people in person. Don't get me wrong, I'm the first one to want to stay at home, but there's just no replacing in-person interactions.

This inbound sales and marketing system seemingly creates gold from thin air because it is a value-based system that gives far more often than it asks. Because we continue to consistently provide value for free, our audience naturally thinks of us first when they might need help from a paid product or service offering we provide.

This eventually leads to business for us because we're building relationships with people at scale. And that's powerful. Most people don't have the patience to develop this type of system; it can take years to form. But those who stick with it and build a sales and marketing machine based on value and relationships will reap the rewards for a long time. This applies to both individuals and companies alike, and the converse is also painfully true.

What If You Build It and They Don't Come?

Silicon Valley is one of the most revered places in the world to start businesses. It's where Google, Apple, Intel, and Facebook are now headquartered. It's also where most startups go to die. In many cases, the cause of death is poor sales and marketing.

In many places around the world, people believe that a great product alone will make people get their wallets out, ready to buy: "If you build it, they will come." But that couldn't be further from the truth. There are countless stories of great product companies that had to shut down because their growth stalled.

Those who stick with it and build a sales and marketing machine **based on value and relationships will reap the rewards for a long time.**

- Beepi, a website that brought together car buyers and used-car sellers, ran out of money after raising $150 million. It was previously valued at $560 million.

- Yik Yak, an anonymous social media app, raised $73 million and was valued at $400 million before closing up shop.

- Jawbone, a pioneer in wearable devices, had to liquidate its assets after raising $1 billion. It was valued at $3 billion at its peak and had a chance to completely dominate the product category it had created. Instead, Fitbit overtook it and stole the category.

A well-known venture capitalist in Silicon Valley, Dave McClure, once said, "It's laughable we worship Silicon Valley as some kind of mecca for startups given how functionally illiterate the Valley is at marketing." If a company does not know how to market or sell consistently, it will fail. That's why many startups now have "growth teams" specifically designed to focus on these areas.

The same approach to marketing and sales applies to real life. Why do most people revere Michael Jordan as the greatest basketball player of all time? Because he was constantly out there marketing and selling his greatness on national television. Why did you become attracted to someone? It was because of the way they presented themselves. Something about them "sold" you on them.

Everything around you is being marketed and sold to you all the time. It's your desire that causes you to eventually take an action on something. Marketers and salespeople are equipped to capitalize on this. The upshot of all of this? Marketing and sales matter if you want to maximize your life.

From the *Leveling Up* Podcast:
Derek Halpern

I interviewed Derek Halpern of *Social Triggers*, a popular online marketing blog. We talked about how Derek went from being a celebrity gossip columnist (forty million page views in one year) to a corporate employee at a Fortune 100 company to striking it out on his own as an entrepreneur. We discussed the content strategy he used to grow *Social Triggers* from nothing to 70,000 subscribers in just sixteen months. (Today his website has more than 300,000 subscribers.)

Derek talked about the power of marketing and how he uses paid advertising combined with content marketing, which is a form of educating consumers before they buy, to grow his multi-million-dollar business. Even with a large following, Derek religiously studies new marketing and sales strategies and tactics because he understands those two things are competitive advantages. They are superpowers to leverage.

Marketing was how I discovered Derek and, coincidentally, I helped him get a speaking slot at a marketing conference in New York because he's such an effective marketer and entrepreneur.

Remember, you're *always* being marketed to on a daily basis.

You can listen to my interview with Derek Halpern by searching "Leveling Up Derek Halpern" or by going to LevelingUp.com/marketing/derek-halpern-email-subscribers.

Always think about what's in it for *them* before you think about yourself.

Bonus Mini-Interview: Nathan Chan

I interviewed Foundr CEO Nathan Chan, whose successful digital entrepreneur magazine generates millions of dollars in revenue a year (and which has over 2.6 million followers on Instagram). He is the epitome of grit: bootstrapping his company from the start and building its audience.

He is also a gamer. As he told me, "I was a big fan and gamer of *Counter-Strike*. Playing games has helped me become a good problem solver. Building a business is hard—all you do is solve problems every day."

Foundr, as Nathan described it, is "a digital media company that produces entrepreneurial content (magazine, books, blog, video, audio, courses) for founders that are either starting or growing a business." Millions consume its content every month.

I caught up with him to get his story on how important marketing and sales has been to Foundr. "If you have a great product," Nathan told me, "you still need good marketing to get it into the hands of the right people. For our business, marketing is everything." He expanded: "We've been quite strong on social media and content marketing, as content is our core business. From this, we've generated millions of followers on social media and our business turns over multiple millions in revenue per year. The most important thing is, though, that our content has been able to impact so many people on such a large scale, which is the core of our mission at Foundr."

And what about sales? Does it go hand in hand with marketing? "Yes," Nathan said. "Without knowing how to sell, marketing is pointless. Good marketing should always have a strategy in place and behind it, and part of that is linking the marketing initiative back to product or brand, and one day ROI."

One of the biggest advantages that you can gain is through building a brand. This could mean building influence on You-Tube, Twitch, Instagram, and more. If you have influence, you have attention, which means you have leverage. This is how influencers like Kylie Jenner can build a cosmetics empire around her brand. That's marketing and sales.

Sales and marketing are the lifeblood not just for companies but for people. If you know how to sell and market yourself, you'll have an advantage in most situations. And if you decide to start a business, you'll have two of the key skills needed to grow a business.

If you want to win in the long term, you'd better acquire these two superpowers: sales *and* marketing.

You can listen to my interview with Nathan Chan by searching "Leveling Up Nathan Chan" or by going to LevelingUp.com/nathan-chan-foundr-magazine.

GAMIFY YOUR LIFE WITH THESE POWER TIPS

Improving at sales and marketing will magically open doors you never thought possible. The people who lack this power-up are unable to play at the highest levels of life. So, where do you turn to learn about these powers?

- **Seth Godin:** Seth Godin is known as a master marketer who has many bestselling books and also happens to have some of the world's shortest blog posts with millions of readers. He can have a profound effect with only 200 words. His blogs and his books are prime examples of how to stand out in crowded spaces. Read his book *Purple Cow* to learn how you can emulate his success.

- **Neil Patel:** As mentioned earlier, Neil Patel is my podcast co-host and he also happens to be one of the more popular marketing figures online. You can visit his blog at NeilPatel.com to get guides on marketing. He once spent over $30,000 on a single marketing guide—and gave it away for free. That's another example of standing out from other people.

- *The Ultimate Sales Machine* by **Chet Holmes** and *The Sales Acceleration Formula* by **Mark Roberge:** These are two books I require my salespeople to read because they break down the fundamentals of modern sales.

- *Breakthrough Advertising* by **Eugene M. Schwartz:** This book is a classic, and on Amazon copies sell for *hundreds* of dollars. If you want to learn how to write compelling copy that sells, this is the book to read. Although it's old, it's evergreen; I find myself coming back to it at least once a year to refresh my memory on copywriting principles. If you are scrappy, you will find a way to get this book. Be creative. ;)

- **The Boron Letters by Gary Halbert:** The late legendary copywriter wrote these letters to his son while he was in prison. The letters themselves are a great case study on excellent copywriting and serve as a good starting point for any copywriter.

- **Copyblogger:** This is one of the few copywriting blogs I read from time to time. Copywriting is a crucial skill because, at the end of the day, words sell, and if you aren't compelling with your copy, you're not going to be able to sell as much.

- **Learn how to write great headlines:** Study email newsletters or ads that compel you to click on them. Make an entry about them in your favorite note-taking tool and continue to do so. I love saving up great headlines because they serve as templates for when I write my next ad. Why? Because if they compelled me to take an action, they're likely to compel others, too.

- **Create a "swipe library":** Do you ever come across ads that just stop you in your tracks? Do you ever think about why they stop you? These are perfect candidates to add to your swipe library—a file of ads that you like. As you continue to browse the web, save your favorites and then copy the format of these ads for your own uses. For example, if you see an ad headline that says "5 Dead Simple Ways to Get Rid of Acne" and it resonates with you, reuse it for yourself. Your template for your social media headline might then be "6 Stupidly Easy Ways to Grow Your Instagram Followers."

- **Learn public speaking:** Joining a group like Toastmasters will enhance your public speaking ability. If you can speak well in public, you'll become more charismatic and your confidence will skyrocket. If your confidence goes up, you'll be able to sell more! If you've never spoken at an event before, start small and offer to speak for free. You'll gradually advance through the ranks and be invited to speak at larger conferences—and even be offered money to speak.

QUEST: MARK THE MARKETING

△ **YOUR POWER-UP** △
A better understanding of marketing

× **QUEST DEADLINE** ×
2 hours

1 Think about the last three online purchases you made. For each, find the ads those retailers are running. Let's say you bought something from Nike. Go to Google and type "Facebook Ad Library" and then search for "Nike." You'll get a real-life case study of the ads they're running, where they're running them, and the type of messaging that they're using. Do this for each of the brands you bought.

2 Pick out one brand and think about why it resonated with you. A brand usually tells you a unique story. You can use tools such as Ubersuggest and SimilarWeb to find out what keywords they rank for on Google and where they are getting their web and mobile traffic from.

That's marketing in play—messaging and branding that speaks to you. What you just did is known as competitive analysis.

In many ways, marketing and sales is like playing a game. Once you get a taste of it, you'll see what I mean.

Congratulations!
You just got a bonus.

You acquired the **A** power-up from the **GAMER** framework. Acquire all of these power-ups from the book to unlock the framework to help you grow forever.

Go to **LevelingUp.com/a** and enter in password **"A"** to get your power-up bonus.

LEVEL

9

TEAMWORK

NEW! Level 9
acquired!

In progress

"Teamwork is the ability to work together toward a common vision. The ability to direct individual accomplishments toward organizational objectives. It is the fuel that allows common people to attain uncommon results."

ANDREW CARNEGIE

IN MY HIGH SCHOOL YEARS, I played *Counter-Strike* and *Warcraft III* with a broken mindset. Gaming was starting to take off, and at my school, it was actually "cool" to be good at games. Gaming was my ticket to becoming socially accepted with the popular group. I felt that if I had a positive record, I would be considered a "good player" among my friends. While my tactics worked in terms of getting me into my desired social sphere, I totally missed the point of what it meant to be a great gamer: learning.

In *Warcraft III*, I played one-on-one online matches and ran my record to a good start with thirty-two wins and three losses, and then I started to worry. "What if I run into a player better than me? What if I lose five in a row? What would my friends think of me if I had a 32–8 record?"

I was worrying about the vanity of the game, instead of becoming an elite player. I made an unconscious decision to forgo the experience of learning from my defeats and instead focused on short-term status among my friends.

Then I'd start to lose consecutive games until my record no longer looked impressive. I'd start to get scared and then make a brand-new account to recreate the illusion of my skills. I'd run my account up to an impressive record and then promptly start the cycle again—losing consecutive games and making a new account.

In *Counter-Strike*, I did the same thing in public ten-versus-ten games where I'd have the most impressive record. Then I'd get complacent and vainly worry too much about my record rather than playing for the ultimate goal of winning as a team.

In both *Warcraft III* and *Counter-Strike*, I created a bad habit loop that constantly reinforced itself; I wasn't focused on the right quest. That's why I never improved past a certain plateau. It got so bad that some of my friends who had been average players surpassed me and made fun of me.

My experience playing *World of Warcraft* was a sharp contrast from the two games that I plateaued at because my quest was to help make my team the best in our region. With the right quest in place and the right team marching in sync, we were able to dominate. We all woke up at the same time each day, we communicated with each other constantly, and we even ate together virtually!

How about the best gamers in the world? The top *Counter-Strike* or *League of Legends* clans have coaches who guide them, and they sleep at the same time and eat together to build a bond. Even solo gamers consistently practice and live-stream themselves to hold themselves accountable to a certain standard of play.

As a kid, I remember watching a Chinese movie where a kung fu master instructed his pupil to break one chopstick. The pupil broke it with ease. Then the kung fu master took out a large group of chopsticks and told his pupil to give breaking those a shot. Not one broke.

Why? Strength in numbers.

To be a part of
a great team,
**you first must
commit to
showing up.**

Most of the games I played during my competitive days required some level of teamwork to be elite. This worked for me—I often found myself more engaged when I was working as part of something larger than myself.

What Makes a Great Team?

Because of my experience as a team player, whenever I observe great teams, I always wonder how they came together. How did they become so accomplished? Why did a group of great players join up? How do they stay consistently good? How do they practice?

Guy Kawasaki, former chief evangelist at Apple, pointed out in an interview that "Steve Jobs [had] a saying that A players hire A players, B players hire C players, and C players hire D players. It doesn't take long to get to Z players. This trickle-down effect causes bozo explosions in companies."

Great teams become well known for the great work they do. Why do they do great work? Because they are built with A-player talent. In *World of Warcraft*, our guild, Vicious Cycle, was always defeating the toughest bosses well before any other guilds because of our work ethic and talent. Our guild leader would call us at three a.m. on our cell phones and tell us to go on raids; our rivals would not get a chance to defeat the bosses before we did. That's not all: our guild leader also wanted us to be the top PvP guild on the server, which meant being the top dog in combat versus *any* other guild. He wanted total dominance over all facets of the game. If we weren't waking up early in the morning to defeat bosses, we were training hard in scrimmages.

Regardless of whether we're talking about a game, life, or business, that's a work ethic to which most people aren't willing to commit. But that's what made our team stand out from the rest. We had a team of A players.

As Helen Keller said, "Alone we can do so little; together we can do so much."

Being an introvert, I typically gravitate toward doing things alone. That's why the type of characters I used to pick in games had strong solo capabilities—so I wouldn't need to rely on anyone else. And although I became pretty powerful on my own, there was always a ceiling that kept me from the true height of my game: I couldn't kill the top bosses to get the best items. That required a team. And not just any team—accomplishing that goal required the *best* team.

In *World of Warcraft*, our team logged absurd hours, playing into the wee hours of the morning every single day. We're talking at least ten hours daily. It was a job—we were expected to be on at a certain time to start raids. It was a job we all enjoyed because the game was incredible.

To be a part of a great team, you first must commit to showing up. Then you must show you have what it takes to perform at the team's level.

Great teams have great players who tend to inspire their teammates in different ways. Basketball legend Kobe Bryant was known for getting up at three or four a.m. to practice and for being the last to leave a practice. Former basketball player Jay Williams once came to practice for a game four hours early with the goal of making 400 shots before going back to the locker room to rest for the game against Kobe's Lakers. When he walked onto the court, he saw Kobe drenched in sweat, already practicing. Jay practiced for an hour and a half. When he finished, he still heard the ball bouncing. Bryant didn't finish for another twenty-five minutes. During the game, Kobe scored forty points. After the game, Jay asked Kobe why he was in the gym for so long. Kobe said he saw him come in and

The greatest performers in the world all need to be **surrounded by great people to truly make an impact.**

wanted him to know that "no matter how hard you work, I'm willing to work harder than you." Bryant's competitiveness elevated his team's play during practice and that ultimately helped him win five NBA titles with the Los Angeles Lakers.

What Are Your Core Values?

Look at all the teams that you admire. What are their key characteristics or traits? What makes them so special?

A good team almost always has core values that determine how they do things. Online shoe retailer Zappos is famous for its values, posted on its site:

- Deliver WOW through service
- Embrace and drive change
- Create fun and a little weirdness
- Be adventurous, creative, and open-minded
- Pursue growth and learning
- Build open and honest relationships with communication
- Build a positive team and family spirit
- Do more with less
- Be passionate and determined
- Be humble

I used to think core values were a bunch of fluff. As I got older and a little wiser, I realized I've always had certain core values that helped me gravitate toward teams that aligned with my work style.

I highly recommend reading Zappos CEO Tony Hsieh's book *Delivering Happiness*. It's about building a great company focused on culture. Even if you aren't trying to start a business, his book will show you how to be a great contributor to whatever team you're on.

With my marketing agency, Single Grain, we get to work with some of the most notable brands in the world. And that's not because of any single person. It's because of the team.

Here are Single Grain's core values:

- **Growth.** We must each consistently strive to grow in different ways. We'll do anything to avoid stagnation.

- **Long-term vision.** We must avoid short-termism and focus on the long-term impact we will make on the world.

- **Integrity.** We must operate in good faith and not harm anybody.

- **Tenacity.** We must be relentless and power through walls to get to the next level. Most people give up right when they're about to reach success; we'll go the distance.

- **Accountability.** We must own our failures and successes as individuals and as a team.

- **Creativity.** We will express our creativity to the world through our passionate curiosity.

Core values are great for setting the foundation, but teams also need to be taken care of since they are living, breathing organisms. For example, when the COVID-19 pandemic hit, we immediately issued a small stipend to our team weeks before lockdown. We also had cookies delivered with other small treats plus MasterClass accounts so the team can learn subjects they're interested in. We hire individual coaches for top performers and try to get team members to continually educate themselves. It's the little things that go a long way.

Bill Gates once said that Microsoft was built on the shoulders of its first twenty people. Think about it for a second: you're only as strong as your weakest link. This is why the business of sports is ruthless: once an athlete's performance drops, they're going to be cut or traded.

If you want to do great things in life, you're going to need to be part of a great team. The greatest performers in the world all need to be surrounded by great people to truly make an impact.

From the *Leveling Up* Podcast: Robert Glazer

On the *Leveling Up* podcast, Robert Glazer (also known as Bob) talked about how he scaled his company, Acceleration Partners, from a few team members to over 150 in a short time period. The number-one reason for the growth? Bob's relentless focus on culture and team building. A team is only as good as its people, and building a winning culture keeps people happy when they come into work. A good culture means investing for the long term and taking care of people— something that's easy to say but hard to do consistently.

When Bob spoke at an entrepreneurial master's program that I attended, he talked about how his company only had a few employees for a number of years before he finally started to focus on the culture of the company. Consequently, his revenue and team size exploded. That only happened because he focused intently on making sure that he had the best possible team.

You can listen to my interview with Robert Glazer by searching "Leveling Up Robert Glazer" or by going to LevelingUp.com/growth-everywhere-interview/robert-glazer-acceleration-partners.

GAMIFY YOUR LIFE WITH THESE POWER TIPS

- As an entrepreneur, I participate in groups such as Entrepreneurs' Organization (EO) and Young Presidents' Organization (YPO). These business groups allow me to interact with like-minded people who are trying to change the world. I often get insights that would've taken me years to learn on my own. You'll be amazed by what you're able to accomplish by being teamed up with like-minded individuals. Even if you don't yet have a business, you could start a private group of peers on Facebook.

- If you can, try to find a mentor. A mentor can be someone who has done what you're trying to do. When I started to learn marketing, I read this one blog daily. I emailed the blog owner with questions and with offers to help, and eventually we ended up meeting in person. He later mentored me and we became partners on multiple ventures. His name is Neil Patel—my cohost of *Marketing School*.

- Here's a template that you can use to reach out to a mentor. Let's say you noticed that your ideal mentor could be doing better on social media. Package your ideas in a short email or direct message:

  Hi [Name],

  My name is [your name] and I'm a fan—just wanted to provide some feedback to help you grow faster on social media. I think you could:

  [Short sentence 1]

[Short sentence 2]

I know you're probably busy so I'm happy to do it for you for free if you're open to it.

[Your name]

- If you are trying to start a business from scratch, meet up with people and host "masterminds." Search online for "mastermind dinners PDF" to learn how to arrange one. (You'll likely find my friend Jayson Gaignard's PDF as the first result; he's a pioneer in this space.) I can unequivocally say that without these peer groups, I wouldn't have been able to save one of my businesses from the abyss. Here's a template to use when guests introduce themselves:

Hi everyone. Thanks for joining tonight. I just wanted to go through a few housekeeping items before we chow down on food. First, we're going to introduce ourselves. Please keep yours to under one minute so we can get around the room. Here's the format:

1. Your name
2. What you do
3. One thing you'd like to give
4. One thing you'd like to get

I'll circulate everyone's information after dinner so we can stay connected. I'll go first to get things started and we'll move clockwise.

- Pro tips for hosting a mastermind dinner: Have people keep their cell phones on silent and ideally keep them away. Only invite six to ten people. A circular dining table is the best to foster one group conversation. Too many conversations at once is a distraction. The key thing is to make sure the people you invite are like-minded. If you have eight people and four are entrepreneurs and the other four are interns, it's not going to be a good value balance for everyone involved. It's your job to curate these gatherings to the maximum benefit of others. Remember time is the most important asset we all have; you want to be respectful of it.

- I recently started throwing monthly happy hour events, in addition to monthly dinners. Being the connector has its benefits and pays dividends down the road. Even if you end up paying the bill, the rewards for hosting come back tenfold because of the connections you're able to make. Remember it's all about building relationships. In some cases, you can just invite a group of friends out and have everyone split the bill. Everyone has their own way of running these kinds of meet-ups. Pro tip: if you want to get really creative, you can pitch companies to sponsor these events!

- Make a list of your favorite teams. They could be gaming, sports, or any type of team! Then write down the similarities and differences between the teams in two columns. Circle which traits you want to embody and make these your criteria for choosing who you want to work with.

- You can only get so far soloing. I personally loved to solo in games, but being alone capped my potential. It was only when I joined the elite teams that I got to see and experience things I never would have experienced by myself. There's a certain responsibility that comes with being a top performer on a team, and it motivates you to continue to work harder.

- Read *The Goal* by Eliyahu M. Goldratt. It's a book that Jeff Bezos, CEO of Amazon, requires his executives to read. It's about the theory of constraints and why building a great team or having great systems in place is critical to the success of any organization.

QUEST: BUILD YOUR GUILD

△ **YOUR POWER-UP** △
A top team for your adventures

✕ **QUEST DEADLINE** ✕
14 days

FOR THIS QUEST, you are going to create a peer group so you can learn the power of hosting a mastermind.

1 Create a list of your personal core values and what you hope to accomplish in the next five years. For example, some of my core values are growth, long-term vision, and tenacity.

2 Make a list of five people you know who share similar core values and ambitions. As I said in the Power Tips, keep in mind that you want your guests to be around the same level, so there's minimal imbalance in value exchange.

3 Send your invites out!

4 Put together an agenda of what you hope to accomplish from the meeting. For example, I used to have a marketer's mastermind where we would start with dinner, then people would give updates, and one person would be in the "hot seat" where the group gives them advice on a problem they're facing. Then it rotates to other people. If you need a

template, use the Jayson Gaignard example I shared above. Set a consistent time to meet once a month. Make sure people know that there are consequences for missing multiple meetings (so they take it seriously).

5 It will start out a little rough, but you will get better at hosting these events over time and as you get better, the group will gain more value and you'll have your own informal board of directors.

LEVEL

10

MEDITATIONS

NEW! Level 10
acquired!

In progress

"If you are distressed by anything external, the pain is not due to the thing itself, but to your estimate of it; and this you have the power to revoke at any moment."

MARCUS AURELIUS

MY FELLOW GAMERS, do you remember that feeling when you almost finished a difficult level but painfully fell short because you made a careless error? Do you remember feeling upset and maybe even shouting at the screen?

Or perhaps you were playing a five-versus-five shooting game and it was down to just you and one opposing player to win an important match, but you were narrowly defeated with a "lucky" shot?

Scenarios like this often happened in my gaming career. Sometimes, I'd lose to someone I perceived to be inferior competition and I'd slam my keyboard, curse, and rage quit. Then I'd log back on, but my performance would spiral downward because I was not in a mental position to compete at a high level.

I remember a time in college when I was playing Texas Hold'em and one of my friends was at the table, too. We were two broke college students scraping by. The casino we frequented gave players the chance to win a mini-jackpot if they had a full house beaten by a four of a kind or better. For example, if you had AAAKK (aces full of kings) and you were beaten by AAAAQ (four of a kind aces), you would win $1,000 *as the loser*. The winner got $500, and the rest of the table got $150 each. However, there was one caveat: the jackpot could be killed by an "unqualified" hand if it was shown.

To make a long story short, we were in a jackpot hand, and my friend had a hand that I knew would kill the jackpot. I had a full house (AAA77) and I knew my opponent had four of a kind aces (AAAAQ), so I was desperately trying to get my friend to fold.

Unfortunately, he didn't listen to me and the jackpot was deemed invalid. After the hand, he was full of regret and tried to apologize but I didn't care. I lit into him at the table because his stubbornness cost everyone at the table money. I wouldn't let go of it on the car ride home. I stayed frustrated and angry about the situation for the next few days because, as a young college student, I desperately needed the money. That money was the world to me.

This type of scenario happened to me in business as well. In fact, the marketing agency I own, Single Grain, was a company I took over due to uncontrollable changes that search engines made in their algorithms. The changes were so drastic that Single Grain had to shift its business model a few times, lay off employees, and completely rebuild from the ground up. When I started, the company had five partners. But it got so difficult that eventually the other four partners left the business and I had to figure it out my own. In the early days of the struggle, I would lose my cool with employees and place the blame on their shoulders. I blamed everybody else and did not take responsibility for my actions. I was moody, angry, and unpleasant to be around.

When I reflect back on Google changing its algorithms or me losing the mini-jackpot, there's only one thing I would change: my attitude. Everything else was completely out of my control, but I lost control of the one thing that I had 100 percent influence over.

Budget Your Worrying Better

Remember we can't control what happens around us, but we can control our reaction to the situation. Those who lose their cool often are misallocating their energy.

How often do you worry about things that are out of your control? Let's list a few potential examples:

- The weather
- Aircraft turbulence
- People arguing about politics on social media
- Traffic

And how often does it help you to worry about these things? Almost never, right?

That's because worrying is a state of suffering (and inaction) and it takes away from your energy without you being able to do anything about the situation.

So, rather than focusing on things that are out of your control, what if you reallocated that energy to focus on the things that are well within your control?

- Instead of worrying about how fit someone else looks, eat healthier and exercise more.

- Instead of worrying about being rejected by someone you're attracted to, ask them out. If that fails, ask someone else out. You'll gain so much experience over time that eventually people will start saying yes. And if they say no, is that such a bad thing?

We can't control what happens around us, **but we can control our reaction to the situation.**

- Instead of envying someone's success, do everything you can to learn. Work for free for a similar business and consume as much information as you can to gain an edge.

By working on the things well within your control, you'll make progress.

I mentioned that when I played the MMORPG *EverQuest*, I had always looked up to the top guild on the server but never thought I was qualified enough to play with them. I spent most of my time soloing—until I decided that in order to be doing the most interesting things, I had to be with the most interesting guild. That's when I made a concerted effort to reach out every day and offer to help them.

It first started with me joining groups of six to do mini-raids on dungeons. Then when I became friends with enough of them, I made the request to see if one of them would recommend me. That eventually led to me being invited to go on forty- to sixty-person dragon raids, where I performed well.

In the middle of all this, a wrench was thrown into my plans. There was one guy in the guild who didn't like me, and I believe this was because he saw me as a threat. We both happened to play the same class, druid, so he saw me as encroaching on his territory. But I was able to get around that by consistently offering to help him, and we eventually became friends. Problem solved.

Then I got into the guild.

Let's review what was not in my control:

- A rival who disliked me on the team that I wanted to join
- The team's opinion of me
- Limited slots open for new members

Let's review what was in my control:

- Offering to help with smaller efforts
- Having a great attitude (which led to being a part of larger raids)
- Being friendly and helpful to the person who didn't like me

By focusing on only the things I could control, my mind felt more at ease. The little actions I took eventually led to my acceptance.

How to Be a Stoic

The practice of focusing on what you can control is a major component of the philosophy known as stoicism. This, to me, is a practical form of philosophy.

The basic idea is that as individuals, we ultimately can only rely on ourselves and our responses to external events. This is exemplified by a quotation from Epictetus: "In life our first job is this, to divide and distinguish things into two categories: externals I cannot control, but the choices I make with regard to them I do control. Where will I find good and bad? In me, in my choices."

Former U.S. president Theodore Roosevelt said, "What such a man needs is not courage but nerve control, cool headedness. This he can get only by practice." When Roosevelt spent eight months in the treacherous Amazon jungle, the two books he brought with him were based on stoicism: Marcus Aurelius's *Meditations* and Epictetus's *Enchiridion*. Other world leaders such as Bill Clinton and Wen Jiabao, the former premier of China, also regularly read Aurelius's *Meditations*. Stoicism should constantly be a work in progress, and one good way to keep it top of mind is to re-read books from the greatest philosophers to ever live, such as Aurelius.

Marcus Aurelius was not just a philosopher, though. He ruled over the Roman Empire when it was a superpower. Aurelius had to fend off invaders, make sure the people of his empire were happy, and deal with cunning politicians who were looking to take his place.

He originally wrote *Meditations* as a book of lessons he learned. The key point of the book? Although he had a million things flying at him every day, Aurelius realized that to be effective he just needed to focus on the key things only he could change. Everything else was simply a distraction.

I interviewed bestselling author Ryan Holiday on the *Leveling Up* podcast and we briefly touched on stoicism. Ryan wrote a book called *The Obstacle Is the Way*, which goes into detail on the benefits of stoicism, complete with real-life examples.

When I asked Ryan to define stoicism, he replied, "Stoicism is a philosophy that believes we don't control the world around us, we control only how we respond. Stoicism is a philosophy that provides exercises and insights on how to respond. How to respond well to this world in which we are relatively powerless."

"There's a reason," Ryan continued, "that it's popular with everyone from Marcus Aurelius, who was the emperor, the most powerful man in the world, to Epictetus, who was a former slave, who was actually banished from Rome by a different emperor. It's this philosophy that really suits itself to the powerful and the powerless because it tells us, 'Hey, I'm just a guy. I didn't make this world, but I got to figure out the rules and I got to make the most of them.'"

From the *Leveling Up* Podcast: Brian Dean

Brian Dean, also known as Backlinko, created an SEO blog when it was no longer novel to do so. In fact, the category was already saturated and competitive. But against all odds, with his unique approach, Brian was able to build a successful seven-figure business.

After explaining his academic background in nutrition and how his original life plan involved becoming an employee for someone else, Brian told me how he found himself out of a job and without any prospects. With nothing else to do, he found himself hanging out in his parents' basement reading *The 4-Hour Workweek*. He'd never considered entrepreneurship before, but Tim Ferriss's book opened Brian's eyes to a way in which he could start a niche website to support himself when he didn't have any other job prospects.

By focusing on only what he could control and taking matters into his own hands, Brian became an entrepreneur. He defied the odds and powered through to create a blog that has over 300,000 viewers a month.

———

You can listen to my interview with Brian Dean by searching "Leveling Up Brian Dean" or by going to LevelingUp.com/seo/backlinko-brian-dean-build-traffic-seo.

GAMIFY YOUR LIFE
WITH THESE POWER TIPS

- Earlier I mentioned trying a meditation app, such as Headspace or Calm. I know many people are skeptical, but just give it a shot for ten days and see what happens. There's a reason I'm mentioning it twice!

- Make a list of all the things that anger and/or frustrate you. Now make a list of all the good being angry about them has done. Cross off all the things you have done about them that you could have done without getting angry. Now make a list of all the harm it has done. Then ask yourself if it is helpful to be angry about things.

- To take it a step further, write down what you'd love to say to someone you're in conflict with right now. Write it all down but do not send the note. This practice can be a great way to relieve yourself and control your emotions. It's what President Abraham Lincoln used to do when he was upset.

- After you finish writing the note, go for a walk. A walk goes a long way to clearing the mind and calming down heightened emotions.

- Next time you lose your cool, write down why you lost control and what you could've done differently. By writing down the reasons, you'll be able to slowly learn from your errors.

- Read or re-read writing on stoicism, especially Marcus Aurelius's *Meditations*. If it could help an emperor and a slave, it can help you.

QUEST: REFRAME

△ **YOUR POWER-UP** △
Emotional control

✕ **QUEST DEADLINE** ✕
Ongoing quest (keep doing this)

THIS IS AN on-the-spot challenge you can do again and again.

1 Write down something that upsets you or gets in your way.

2 Now write down how you can turn it into a positive with a change of perspective. Yes, you already know how—you just have to let yourself see it and do it.

The next time something frustrates or upsets you, do this little quest again!

For example, I used to get flustered when I felt people underestimated me, and I desperately wanted to prove to them that I was capable by arguing on the spot. But I learned that trying to fight fire with fire almost never helped because I was so consumed with anger that I struggled to think clearly. Instead, I learned to reframe being underestimated as a positive thing—because my attitude is one thing I can control. Plus it helped me release my anger.

Being underestimated can be good because people won't try their best against you. And when you finally prove to them that you were worthy all along, it'll feel even better because you were able to shift their impression from negative to positive. Being constantly underestimated is also an advantage because it forces you to continue to sharpen your skills, so you'll never get too lazy.

See how I changed something that used to drive me nuts into an advantage?

If you're able to reframe situations, it'll change the way you react to them. The more control you have over your reactions, the more at peace you'll feel. The more at peace you feel, the better work you'll do.

Congratulations!
You just got a bonus!

You acquired the **M** power-up from the **GAMER** framework. Acquire all of these power-ups from the book to unlock the framework to help you grow forever.

Go to **LevelingUp.com/m** and enter in password "**M**" to get your power-up bonus.

LEVEL

11

FOCUS

NEW! Level 11
acquired!

In progress

"People think focus means saying yes to the thing you've got to focus on. But that's not what it means at all. It means saying no to the hundred other good ideas that there are. You have to pick carefully. I'm actually as proud of the things we haven't done as the things I have done."

STEVE JOBS

HAVE YOU EVER heard the phrase "jack of all trades, master of none"?

It's something I struggled with a lot in gaming. Although I always strived to be great in any game I played, I often found myself drawn in envy to the shiniest object. For example, in *World of Warcraft*, when I played as a hunter, I would stare at mages from my guild and imagine myself in their shoes, throwing fireballs at the toughest bosses. I thought to myself, "Man, I wish my character was as interesting as theirs." I would then switch from being a top hunter on my server into a newbie mage, which meant throwing away my hard-won progress.

This didn't stop with the type of character I played, either. When I'd start to hit my stride in one game, I'd switch to another up-and-coming game. In areas where I had no talent, such as basketball or volleyball, I'd constantly switch between games and never practiced. It's no surprise that I never got good at any one sport.

My poor habits followed me into the business world. At conferences or networking events, I would hear of some new business model that someone else was "printing money" with and I'd get envious and try to do the same thing. This is referred to as "shiny object syndrome," and many entrepreneurs fall victim to it. Don't be one of them.

The time and effort it takes to adjust to a new course of action is known as switching cost. In a nutshell, switching costs are those you incur as a result of bouncing from one thing to another, be it a brand, a supplier, a product, or an entire business model.

Here's one concept you can take to the grave: think of success as a circle and yourself as a dot in the center. To reach success, you need to reach any point on the edge of the circle. Now imagine you are moving north. Then you decide to switch and go south. Then you see a new opportunity and decide to go west. Then another opportunity surfaces and you go north again. Then east. Then south. Then north again. If you keep switching, you'll never reach success.

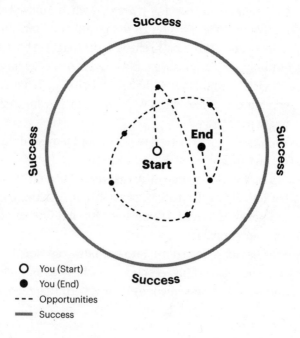

And that's how it works in real life: focus on one area until you reach success before trying to do something else. Confucius said that "the man who chases two rabbits catches neither." So do your best to focus!

What's Your First Love?

Although I have multiple businesses today, I stay in my lane: marketing. I love creating content and educating people. To me, it feels like I have a superpower that allows me to magically enhance any business. I love pulling different levers and then seeing things grow as a result. It's deeply satisfying. This book is the perfect example. I'm writing this sentence on an airplane while everyone else is asleep. No normal person would do that unless they felt genuine enjoyment and excitement. To me? It's a game!

As I gain more life experience, I focus on the areas that I'm good at while continually trying to take things off my plate that I'm not good at. Focus is key to success.

When Google first started, it focused on being good at one thing: search. When Amazon first started, it focused on creating a great ecommerce experience for its customers by selling books online. When Uber first started, it focused on ridesharing. Sure, these big companies do many different things today, but they started with one thing—at which they were really good. Grind as hard as you can on one thing and then once you're set, feel free to branch off into newer opportunities.

I remember interviewing Cal Newport, TED speaker and author of *So Good They Can't Ignore You*, on my *Leveling Up* podcast. He said one driver of success is doing "deep work," meaning you focus without distraction on a demanding task.

Focus is key to success.

When you're in a state of deep work, it can sometimes feel unpleasant, but if you can cultivate this practice, you'll do exceptionally well. Deep work is similar to the concept of flow, which is when you feel like you're "in the zone" and "locked in" on what you're working on. Flow is something we all have experienced, but perhaps you have not previously defined it for yourself. It's a gratifying experience and I encourage you to find out what kind of environment most easily puts you into a state of flow.

When you start to see the fruits of your labor grow, double down on what you've been doing. Often, people focus on one thing, start to see some success, and then *move on* to something else. But does that make any sense?

In today's world, where attention is harder than ever to maintain, it's more important than ever to lock in on the important things and cut out the distractions. If you see something working, put more fuel on that fire. That's a fundamental pillar in modern-day marketing.

Focus, double down, and repeat.

From the *Leveling Up* Podcast: Ramit Sethi

Ramit Sethi has an audience of over one million readers a month and sells training programs to help people start their businesses. His first book, *I Will Teach You to Be Rich*, became a *New York Times* bestseller and impacted my life when I was twenty-three years old. How? By teaching me how to focus on money-saving tactics such as index fund investing and picking the right credit cards, bank accounts, and more. Ramit helped me unlearn financial advice from my parents and uncles (who were usually wrong).

Ramit is known for his relentless focus. He has had single weeks where he generated over $5 million in revenue. But all that success came from one simple concept—sticking to what he knew best without getting distracted by shiny objects around him.

Ramit only focuses on a few key activities at which he *knows* he is exceptional. I've followed his content for close to ten years, and over all that time, I can see that he still just focuses on what he's good at: copywriting and book writing. He has dabbled in other mediums, such as Instagram, but his primary focus is still on his bread and butter. In the last decade, a variety of other growth channels, such as Facebook advertising, have surfaced and Ramit was smart to see the opportunity in the channels and *hire* experts to work with him, instead of trying to do it all on his own.

It takes extreme self-control to only focus on a certain area when there are hundreds of other opportunities dangling in the air. Those who can maintain focus have an edge on their counterparts.

You can listen to my interview with Ramit Sethi by searching "Leveling Up Ramit Sethi" or by going to LevelingUp.com/growth-everywhere-interview/ramit-sethi-i-will-teach-you-to-be-rich.

GAMIFY YOUR LIFE
WITH THESE POWER TIPS

- Take a high-touch approach to the skills you want to develop. In his book *The Talent Code*, Daniel Coyle talks about the success of Brazilian football players and why people around the world seem to think that Brazilians naturally have more football talent. Beyond any innate talent, what Brazilians do is get a lot more touches on the football because they play on very small fields compared to the giant football stadiums people are used to seeing. A smaller field leads to more touches, and more touches equals more repetition, which equals more built-up myelin (see the following quest!). That's part of the reason why Brazilians are so good.

- Use the Pomodoro technique, which is the concept of allocating twenty-five-minute "sprints" for each task you have in front of you. For example, if I have seven tasks for the day, I'll tackle task #1 for twenty-five minutes, then take a five-minute break, then jump to task #2 and repeat. Don't be too hard on yourself to get all your Pomodoros done in one day. Often only getting a few done can move the needle for your long-term vision. As I'm writing this, I'm using a Pomodoro app to keep me on track.

- Do an audit of your time. Use a tool like RescueTime to track how you're using your computer. RescueTime sits in the background and gives you a weekly summary of how you used your computer. For your mobile device, you can use an app called Instant to track how you're behaving on your phone. An app called Gyroscope will integrate with RescueTime and a bunch of other productivity apps to track just how effective you are. Use functions such as iPhone's Screen Time to track how often you are using certain apps.

- Focus on *one* thing. I recommend reading *The ONE Thing* by Gary W. Keller and Jay Papasan (also available as an audiobook). It advises that you should focus on *one* big thing for each day/week/month/year. In truth, it's often only one big thing that is going to drive exponential results. Most people focus on getting a bunch of tasks done, but you're far better at taking control of your time and being deliberate with it by focusing on one key thing.

- Block out time for yourself and say no more. Sounds counterproductive, right? The reality is the best thinkers in the world take time to strategize and think. Bill Gates used to think that having his schedule packed to the brim was the sign of a successful CEO—until he met Warren Buffett. Warren Buffett keeps his schedule in a tiny booklet with him every day. His week? Almost completely empty. Buffett famously said, "You've gotta keep control of your time, and you can't unless you say no. You can't let people set your agenda in life."

- Peter Drucker, author of *The Effective Executive* and *Managing Oneself,* said that one of the hardest things to do is to figure out what you are good at and how to focus on it. He wrote about a concept called feedback analysis: you audit all the big decisions you've made in life over a two- to three-year span. By examining these choices, you can see what experiments worked and what didn't. Then you'll know your strengths and weaknesses. All you need to do from there is double down on your strengths and you're off to the races.

Focus, repeat, and progress. **Rinse and repeat.**

QUEST: ADD MYELIN

I USED TO think that talent was something set in stone. After understanding what myelin is, I feel that almost anything is possible.

Myelin is a fatty substance that surrounds your nervous system's "wires." Think of it as insulation wrapping around a wire to make it fatter and fatter. As you build up a skill, you wrap more myelin around your wires: you become more skilled. This is how athletes perform seemingly superhuman feats when it becomes second nature to them. This is how the Brazilian football players Daniel Coyle wrote about build up their talent. We're going to take that concept and build it for you.

1 Think about one skill you want to cultivate. Is it cooking? Basketball? Drawing?

2 Put together a plan to fix one specific thing. For example, if I want to become a better free throw shooter, I might start with making twenty-five free throws a day.

3 Make a plan to gradually ramp up your daily goal, then follow it. For example, go up to fifty free throws a day for a week. As

you extend your quest, make it seventy-five for a week, then 100, and so on. Kobe Bryant would shoot 800 shots before an Olympic practice as part of his workout.

4 Measure your progress. You can use Google Sheets for free to do this. For example, in each row of the spreadsheet, I'd have the date, how many shots I took, and how many I made to give me a percentage. What gets measured gets managed.

This concept applies to virtually anything you want to do. Focus, repeat, and progress. Rinse and repeat.

Your initial quest is to do this for a week to get started. Your extended quest is the next month. Your ongoing quest is . . . as long as it takes you to beat the boss!

LEVEL

12

ENDURANCE

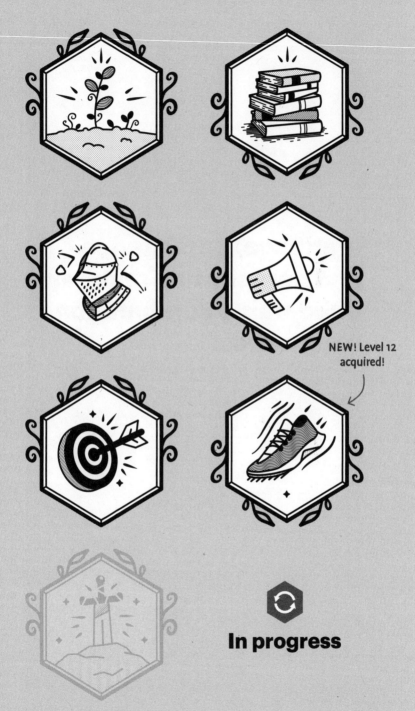

NEW! Level 12 acquired!

In progress

"Patience, persistence, and perspiration make an unbeatable combination for success."

NAPOLEON HILL

WHEN I COMPETED in poker tournaments in college, there were times when I faced tens of thousands of players. Often, late in the tournament with only a few hundred players left, I got impatient and made a rash decision in a game—and I got knocked out of the running as a result. I couldn't endure the mental taxation.

One time I was playing to qualify for the World Series of Poker Main Event, which is the Super Bowl or Champions League of poker. The Main Event had a $10,000 buy-in, and as a broke college student, I couldn't pay upfront for a seat. Instead, I played an online satellite event, a tournament where the top four players earned entry to the Main Event. I made it to the final five; I only needed to outlast one more player to win a seat at the World Series in Vegas!

For whatever reason, I deviated from my normal tournament play, getting creative to muscle out the others. But the other players figured me out, and I got caught being too aggressive by going all in with a bluff. The result of my impatience? The other four players went to the World Series. I stayed at home.

Fail Early, Fail Often

In business, I've faced failure many times. When I took over the marketing agency, we were basically insolvent. During the recovery phase, so many people quit on me that eventually it was just one employee and myself. I struggled to make payroll and my accounting team had a call with me to suggest it might be time to shut down the business.

The agency is now a thriving company with a strong culture, with clients such as Amazon, Salesforce, Nordstrom, Airbnb, Uber, and more.

For my first podcast, *Leveling Up*, I averaged only nine downloads a day in the first year. To put that initial result in perspective, I spent six hours a week interviewing, editing, and writing the show notes for the podcast, all while trying to save the marketing agency from collapsing.

In the second year of my podcast, I had a paltry thirty downloads a day. Then in the third year, it shot up to 3,333 downloads a day with a total of 2.5 million all-time downloads. This led to my second podcast, *Marketing School*, which now has over thirty million downloads and averages one million downloads per month.

I give you these examples to show you that all good things take time to manifest. Most people aren't willing to endure the pain and almost always default to what's easy. That's why most people are most people.

Legendary American football coach Bill Belichick of the NFL's New England Patriots is known for his genius strategic and tactical mind. One tactic in his repertoire is deferring when the team has the option of receiving the ball or waiting until the second half to receive. This gives him the ability to decide how he wants to approach the second half based on the texture of the first half. It also provides the team with the opportunity to score once right before the half and then score again when the second half hits. As of 2020, Belichick has won a total of eight Super Bowl championships. A big part of his success comes from enduring whatever pain comes his way in the first half so he can put the chess pieces in place to win in the second half.

Endure and Build

As human beings, we're always looking for a quick fix. It's just part of our nature. But here's the thing: most of the time, the longer we can delay something, the better.

Compound interest is the classic example. Let's say you invest $10,000 into an index fund, which is a collection of stocks. This fund returns an average of 7 percent a year. After year one, you have $10,700 ($10,000 × 1.07). Not bad, right?

Let's say you decide you don't need that cash for ten years. At the end of ten years, your initial investment will be worth $19,671.51 ($10,000 × $(1.07)^{10}$). If you can leave it alone for twenty years, your initial investment will be worth $38,696.84 ($10,000 × $(1.07)^{20}$). At the end of forty years, your initial investment will be worth $149,744.58 ($10,000 × $(1.07)^{40}$).

Pretty good for just letting your money sit somewhere.

Now let's use the same numbers as above but assume that you continue to contribute $10,000 a year (or $833.33 per month). At the end of forty years, you would have $2,146,095.70. For an extra $390,000 put in, $10,000 at a time, you get an extra $1,996,351.12 at the end.

The power of compound interest is that it stacks over time multiplying into very large amounts by the end. When you keep adding more and more money, the amount multiplies even more. But it takes patience and endurance to get there. Most people don't have that.

The lesson? Don't be most people!

Most people aren't willing to endure the pain and almost always default to what's easy. **That's why most people are most people.**

From the *Leveling Up* Podcast: Mark Newman

On the *Leveling Up* podcast, I spoke with HireVue founder and CEO Mark Newman (he's since sold the company). Despite completing an accelerated international business degree at age twenty, Mark struggled to grow his company as he ran into roadblock after roadblock. But he stuck with it and was able to build the company past $30 million in annual revenue for his on-demand video interviewing service.

The biggest takeaway I got from his interview was that his company was on the brink of failure not once, not twice, but *ten* times. He's seen everything bad that can possibly happen to a business—missing source code, people quitting, finding a "great" hire who flamed out, partnerships that fell apart, and having to raise capital six times because four of those times the company ran out of money. Oh, and the company also lost its servers, with no way to recover them, when a semi-truck ran off the freeway and crashed into its data center.

Despite all of the setbacks that might have sent another startup founder packing, Mark remained patient and never gave up.

"The first five years really sucked," he said, but it made HireVue what it is today. He attributes his positive attitude to the supportive ecosystem of people around him, from loved ones to board members, who pushed him onward.

You can listen to my interview with Mark Newman by searching "Leveling Up Mark Newman" or by going to LevelingUp.com/growth-everywhere-interview/mark-newman.

GAMIFY YOUR LIFE WITH THESE POWER TIPS

- What are you training to get better at right now? Let's use meditation as an example. When I first started to meditate, I had trouble completing the practice for even five minutes because I got so distracted! I built up my practice by meditating for one minute longer until I could go for six minutes, seven minutes, eight minutes, and so on. Try stacking a little extra sauce in your training to gradually to build up your endurance.

- Take your time getting to the top. When I was in my twenties, I thought I needed to reach the pinnacle quickly. What I learned is that "overnight success" actually takes time. Think of the hockey-stick shape of success from level 7.

- Everyone is on a different journey; the only one you need to worry about is yours. It's natural to want to compare yourself, but some people might be twenty years ahead of you and in a different chapter of life, so it's pointless. Comparison can be the thief of your joy.

- If you create a business and it starts to see success, you have two options: continue to pour investments back into the business to fuel growth or take money off the table. As a younger entrepreneur, I chose to pour the investments back into the business. As a result, I see larger returns on my investment over the long term. Endure!

- If you feel you aren't seeing success quickly enough, look at your (or your company's) "unsolicited response rate": people who reach out to you via social media or email to tell you how much they appreciate your work. As long as you continue to receive this kind of feedback, you're on the right track.

- I can't emphasize this enough: have patience. If you're doing good work, great things will eventually happen. Most people give up too early because they aren't willing to go through the pain. Enduring through struggles is required to get away from the beaches of mediocrity.

- To get a better understanding of how to build endurance, learn about antifragility, a coin termed by *Antifragile* author Nassim Nicholas Taleb. The whole idea around antifragility is not only learning to be resilient but learning to improve as you become more resilient. It goes a step beyond endurance. Antifragility means thriving in stress.

QUEST: PLAN OUT THE LONG GAME

△ **YOUR POWER-UP** △
A clear path

✕ **QUEST DEADLINE** ✕
3 days

MAP OUT WHAT you are hoping to accomplish in the next one, five, ten, and twenty-five years. If you haven't done this yet, go back to level 2. Your mission must have specific and time-bound action items so you have a sense of accountability and urgency. Otherwise, nothing gets done.

Your goalposts will change as you continue to level up, but if you don't begin with time-bound goals, you won't know what you are aiming for and it will be difficult to level up without knowing which direction to head.

Once you have defined your goals, work backward from each one to figure out what you need to do to achieve it. For example, let's say you want to donate $1,000 to charity each year. Over a twelve-month period, that means $83.33 per month. What could you do to earn the $83.33 per month? What are you good at that's marketable? What can you sell offline or online? What can you sell that you no longer use?

By setting a time-bound goal and working backward, you can come up with concrete action steps to accomplish it. As long as you keep following this methodology throughout your life—and stay patient about the long term with a sense of urgency about the short term—there is virtually no way you can lose. What do I mean by that? Work swiftly and hard while not expecting any big payoff until maybe five to ten years down the line.

Congratulations!
You just got a bonus!

You acquired the **E** power-up from the **GAMER** framework. Acquire all of these power-ups from the book to unlock the framework to help you grow forever.

Go to **LevelingUp.com/e** and enter in password "**E**" to get your power-up bonus.

LEVEL

13

THIEVERY

NEW! Level 13
acquired!

In progress

"Good artists borrow, great artists steal."

PABLO PICASSO

MOST INVENTIONS AREN'T completely original. Many innovations are actually improvements. Take the car, for example. To get to the car, the wheel had to be invented. Then horses were used to pull carts. Then the combustion engine was invented. Then decades of improvements to get to where we are. And now electric cars.

Apple embraced Pablo Picasso's motto by literally copying inventions—like the mouse, which originally came from Xerox's labs. Facebook built on now-defunct social networks such as Myspace and Friendster. Google "stole" inspiration from prior search engines. Basketball legend Kobe Bryant copied Michael Jordan's moves.

A great example of stealing is Instagram adding its "Stories" function, an imitation of Snapchat, to slow a rival's growth. Snapchat had changed the dynamics of social media with its short-video feature, only to have it copied by Instagram, Facebook, and WhatsApp.

When I was seventeen, Chris Moneymaker won the World Series of Poker championship, which led to the enormous boom in poker. Why? Because Chris Moneymaker was an everyday person who had a day job as an accountant. He was a beginner who happened to win the biggest poker tournament in the world, and that gave everyone hope that they could compete on the highest stage and win millions, just as he did. Because of Moneymaker's victory, my friends and I played almost every day when we were high school seniors. I was the worst of the bunch. My friends often teased me about how I was easy money. That is, until I started to catch on to what my friend Shawn was doing.

A standard bet in our games was maybe thirty to forty cents. But Shawn always bet $1 to $2. He pushed everyone out to take the pots because he was betting more than five times the rest of us most of the time.

That's when it dawned on me: I just needed to steal his aggressive strategy. I went from being called "easy money" to being a constant winner. Not only was I winning hands, but there were plenty of times I'd have everyone's money by the end of the night. It got to the point that my friends said "it was no longer fun" to play with me because of my dominance.

And that worked out just fine. Because once I was no longer being challenged by my friends, I pushed ahead into playing at casinos and online poker so I could continue to hone my craft.

Steal Their Best Moves

In level 2, I talked about *EverQuest*, the game that *World of Warcraft* was modeled on, and how I competed for the title of best of the best for all druids. All my competitors were at the maximum level of 60 (the strongest a character could be), while my character was still at level 55 (significantly weaker).

Before the competition started, I sparred with my guild leader, who was also competing in the tournament. Not only

When you see a problem in the world and you know you want to solve it, you iterate on it. **That's what entrepreneurship is.**

was he at level 60, but he also had far superior weapons and armor to everyone in the field, and he beat me without breaking a sweat. He did this twice in a row.

Because everyone had such a big advantage over me, I thought I had no chance in the tournament—that is, until I actually did.

I lucked out with match pairings and the timing of the matchups. My guild leader went up against one of our rival guild's druids; they were the two best equipped and strongest druids in the tournament. He was defeated and was eliminated from the tournament; it wasn't even close. I was in shock.

Watching that matchup was pivotal. The tactics employed by our rivals were unorthodox, reminding me of my dormant skills learned from first-person shooter games such as *Counter-Strike* and *Quake*. It became clear to me that the reason the rival druid had easily defeated my guild leader was due not to her equipment but to her rapid movements and strafing that made her difficult to effectively react to.

After their match, I copied her tactics and blazed through my first two matches with no problem. Then I came face to face with her. Our battle dragged on for what seemed like an eternity. The match was so close I thought I had lost because my health bar looked like it was completely empty. But in the end, her body was on the ground and I had survived with just 100 health points left, meaning I was merely two hits away from losing the match. The match could have gone either way. I then proceeded into the championship round against her guild leader and won a best of three series by sweeping him in two straight rounds.

My point? There's nothing wrong with taking something and making it better. People might call it stealing, but I like to call it iterating. When you see a problem in the world and you want to solve it, you iterate on it. That's what entrepreneurship is.

When I think about my companies and projects, most of them are iterations of past ideas. ClickFlow fills a need that earlier marketing tools didn't deliver on. *Marketing School* draws inspiration from daily entrepreneurial podcasts. Single Grain is an ad agency that focuses on software companies.

Richard Branson of Virgin exemplifies this: he has started well over 400 companies, and most of his companies are incremental improvements. But in an industry such as airlines, incremental improvements of 10 percent often mean the difference between being number-one or average. Branson took things that were already working and made them better. That's why he's a billionaire.

Kobe Bryant, five-time NBA champion, was said to imitate basketball legend Michael Jordan so extensively that when Jordan was asked who could have beaten him in his prime, he said Kobe Bryant—because he stole all his moves.

Absorb the ideas of others. Steal ethically from all around you. Information is abundant today. All you need to do is take action and continue to iterate every single day.

Sam Walton wrote in his book *Made in America*, "Most everything I've done, I've copied from someone else." Walton founded Walmart.

Stealing Lessons from the *Leveling Up* Podcast

After interviewing over 300 entrepreneurs, what I've learned is that businesses are science projects. They are living, breathing organisms continually evolving over time. This is especially true in the early days of a business. When a business is still new and small, if it makes a mistake, it can change course and quickly adjust.

That's why I love talking to entrepreneurs about their early days. Inevitably, there came a moment for when they had to face life or death in terms of the company. Mark Newman's HireVue almost went bankrupt ten times. Now it's valued at over $1 billion.

How did HireVue get there? By constantly iterating.

Remember my friend Noah Kagan, founder of Sumo and AppSumo? He was an early employee of Facebook—and he got fired because they didn't think he was the right long-term fit. That cost him at least $100 million. Noah found success when he drew inspiration from Groupon and started a deals site (AppSumo) and also created email software (Sumo).

Iterate, iterate, iterate. That's how Noah Kagan and Mark Newman created their success.

When I look at the products and services of the people I interview for my *Leveling Up* podcast, most of them are nothing game-changing. That's no knock on the people creating these products and services—that's just the reality. Most new things are small tweaks on previous inventions. And that's good! As time goes on, things get better and better, and we all have the chance to capitalize on small opportunities for improvement.

My point? People steal all the time. They just don't like to phrase it that way because it sounds illegal. But the sooner you can get over that misconception, the sooner you can focus on iterating on your perfect way of life. Steal away, my friends.

GAMIFY YOUR LIFE WITH THESE POWER TIPS

- **Innovate.** People with internet fame such as Casey Neistat and Gary Vaynerchuk became famous because they do things differently. Casey took vlogging and made it high quality. Gary hired someone to follow him around all day to document his business journey. They improved on existing models and others thought they were worth following. What can you do to make something even better? Make a list of five things that really excite you and pick two that you could combine to create your own unique spin.

- **Iterate.** In order to continually iterate, refer to level 4, Get Reading. Iteration requires you to constantly learn. It's through learning that we're able to reinvent ourselves. Learning provides us with new ideas that lead to inventions that affect the lives of others. How are you continuing to learn?

- **Stay current.** Feedly helps me keep track of the blogs I love most. I follow many entrepreneurship, tech, and marketing blogs to stay on top of trends that then inform my worldview. Checking Feedly first thing in the morning helps me iterate as I start my day.

- **Seek opportunity.** FE International is a company that buys and sells online businesses. I often look at what kind of businesses they are selling for inspiration. I see a company's revenue and if its business model is something worth paying attention to. Because I'm in the marketing niche, I look for tools for sale that compete with some of the best marketing tools out there. Buying a company from FE International and then improving it to be among the top in its field would save me a lot of time and effort, in not having to start from the ground up.

- **Study the competition.** I also like looking at Crunchbase to see which companies have recently been acquired and the acquisition prices. It gives me an indication of where the market is headed. If someone is willing to shell out over a billion dollars for a company, they must think it's worth way more, and I want to understand why.

- **Understand trends.** Dribbble and Behance are designer portfolio sites. I like to look at them for inspiration to see what kind of logos people are designing, what popular styles are trending, and potentially what talent I can recruit. It's an easy way to hire some of the best designers in the world and stay on top of trends that I can incorporate into my own projects.

- **Collaborate with the best.** Land-book is a compilation of some of the best homepage and landing page designs on the internet. I go here to look for inspiration and then to Dribbble find the person who designed the pages.

A lot of the above examples cater to marketing and business because that's the world that I live in. But you can draw inspiration from my framework for your own niche. Inspiration is abundant; you just have to find it.

Absorb the ideas of others. **Steal ethically from all around you.**

QUEST: WHAT DO YOU WANT TO STEAL?

△ **YOUR POWER-UP** △
Stolen treasure—that you make
your own with improvements

× **QUEST DEADLINE** ×
1 day

WHAT'S A SUBJECT you're truly interested in right now? Is it a sport? Cooking? Gardening? Pick a topic and go deep on it. A lot of iteration is based on learning, so you'll have to educate yourself. Here's how.

1   First find where the information is. For example, you can use Reddit and YouTube as a starting point to study home improvement. There are plenty of online communities, forums, and Facebook groups where fanatics hang out.

2   If you want to find the strongest YouTube channel on a topic, you can use a tool like Social Blade to look for the best ones. Find some channels you really like.

3   Pay attention to what strikes you as really cool in the subject area. Think about how you could steal that concept and improve on it—I mean iterate on it! It doesn't matter how good or bad your idea is. What matters is that the wheels are turning in your head.

4 Now write down what action you could actually take to make your idea a reality.

This is how a lot of iteration starts: with planning and taking baby steps.

My cousin learned how to garden just by watching YouTube videos. He went from knowing nothing to having an entire backyard of vegetables that he harvests daily. *Ryan's World*, a YouTube toy review channel, started as an iteration of another review show. As of 2019, that channel has over twenty million subscribers and has collected over $26 million in annual revenue.

LEVEL

14

REPETITION

NEW! Level 14
acquired!

In progress

"A baseball swing is a very finely tuned instrument. It is repetition, and more repetition, then a little more after that."

REGGIE JACKSON

SO NOW THAT you have read this far, you have learned about many of the skills necessary to win at the game of life. What next?

Bestselling author Malcolm Gladwell wrote that it takes 10,000 hours for someone to reach expert status with any skill. And that's not just 10,000 hours of mindlessly practicing. It's practice that focuses on the right things—the aspects that work—that drives people to mastery.

In first-person shooter games such as *Counter-Strike* and *Quake*, we often scrimmaged or practiced with ourselves at set times each week. Sometimes, we even scheduled friendly matches with other teams to stay sharp. In *World of Warcraft*, I often found myself dueling other people one on one to keep my battle skills honed. By doing so, I noticed little tics in how I fought. I fixed those mistakes—or sometimes completely changed my strategy. These seemingly mundane practice sessions taught me how to think on my feet and that proved to be invaluable.

In *WoW*, we often did ten-versus-ten battles with other teams. To create consistency in our team dynamics, we usually played with the same ten people. If someone made a mistake, screaming would be heard over the voice chat app we used.

Seemingly harmless practice matches became high-pressure environments where people cracked. Players who didn't do well in practice were relegated to a lower team to maintain the quality of the A team.

Those who could take the pressure and who had the commitment to get better stayed on the A team. These people reaped the rewards because they could take the feedback, iterate, and communicate exceptionally well. Because of that repetition, any issues we had were identified and solved quickly. When it came time for official, higher-stakes match-ups, we were more than prepared.

Don't get me wrong: these repetitive sessions often became grinds—sometimes to the point I didn't want to play the game anymore—but we all understood that committing to excellence meant doing boring things over and over.

Compare this to business: you look to find a formula that works and then scale it, which just means repeating it over and over. Once you have a model working, you ramp up everything and that's how a business gets big.

When I look at our daily podcast, *Marketing School*, one of the biggest factors in our success I can point to is our relentless drive. The podcast is a daily show that involves two entrepreneurs geeking out on marketing. We have been doing the podcast for years and, to this day, we haven't missed one episode. It doesn't matter if one of us is sick, is having a baby, or has some big event happen—we're always prepared because we know repetition breeds success.

Grind Through the Boredom

The key to success in anything in life is to find something that works and then double down on it. Often that means doing

Repetition breeds success.

seemingly boring, unsexy things such as weekly meetings with my leadership team, recruiting, editing content, and topic ideation. But doing those things is what leads to breakout success. Don't believe me? Just look at Amazon: Jeff Bezos first built an online bookstore and then made it the Everything Store. Facebook first built its social network and then started acquiring other social networks to connect the world. The point is these companies found something that worked and just kept repeating the formula.

Repetition, repetition, repetition.

When I was nine years old, I watched my cousin play the first-person shooter game *Quake*. He often went to his local internet café and played "death matches" where players vied for the top kill-to-death ratio in each game. *Quake* was one of the earliest multiplayer first-person shooter games to catch on, and one of the rising stars of the industry was a guy named Dennis Fong. If you remember from level 5, Dennis not only went on to win many tournaments in different games throughout his career, he also parlayed that success into the world of business.

Dennis started multiple businesses (some of which he later sold) and attributes his competitive mentality to gaming. I interviewed him on the *Leveling Up* podcast and asked how hard he trained during his gaming days. He said it was so grueling that he developed carpal tunnel syndrome. That level of dedication is also what earned him the title of "the Michael Jordan of gaming."

Here's the thing: most high performers *don't* want to wake up early in the morning. They *don't* want to go to the gym consistently. They *don't* want to journal every day. They *don't even* want to floss every day.

But they do it anyway because repetition breeds success. They enjoy the journey and keep doing what most people aren't willing to do. For help tracking these daily fundamental tasks, refer back to our discussion of routines in level 5.

Even the messaging around this book, *Leveling Up*, is something you will see repeated over and over.

From the *Leveling Up* Podcast: Ryan Blair

I interviewed Ryan Blair, a number-one *New York Times*–bestselling author, serial entrepreneur, multi-millionaire, and CEO of ViSalus. He had a tough life growing up in a poor family in Detroit, Michigan; his abusive father was a Vietnam War veteran dealing with that trauma. His father fled after Ryan's school principal reported him to social services. Ryan's family was living in poverty—and that led him to join a gang. Ryan had to fight every single day to prove himself. One time he didn't show up, and someone shot five of his friends. That was when Ryan knew he had to break the vicious cycle.

Things took a positive turn when his stepdad entered the picture. He was a successful entrepreneur who taught Ryan about personal growth, real estate, investing, and value systems. Slowly but surely, Ryan turned his negative habits into positive ones, and he got back on his feet. Eventually he took a company from $6 million in debt to $624 million in revenue. Ryan's story is a roller-coaster ride of emotions and a journey from rock bottom to rock star.

You can listen to my interview with Ryan Blair by searching "Leveling Up Ryan Blair" or by going to LevelingUp.com/growth-everywhere-interview/ryan-blair-visalus.

- As mentioned earlier and to drive the point home, search "tiny habits" on YouTube and learn how to create micro habits that will eventually grow into much bigger habits. For example, if you want to run every day, set the goal as putting on your running shoes and taking at least one step outside. If the habit resonates, your body will naturally want to push harder and harder. The key is starting. Make a list of three new habits you'd like to grow for the next twelve months. It could be exercising daily, flossing, writing, reading, or whatever your heart desires!

Congratulations!
You just got a bonus.

You acquired the **R** power-up from the **GAMER** framework. Go to **LevelingUp.com/r** and enter in password "**R**" to get your power-up bonus.

You now have the complete password for the book bonus. Get to the final chapter to acquire the link. Don't cheat, endure. ;)

QUEST: HABITS = REPETITION

△ YOUR POWER-UP △
Compounding habits that
will give you an edge!

× QUEST DEADLINE ×
7 days

1 Pick one to three habits that you want to cultivate.

A Use a journal or an app such as Way of Life to track your habit streaks.

B Set a repetition goal. For example, you might want to work out seven days in a row. If you are able to hit the goal, set some time of type of reward to treat yourself. Victories should be celebrated!

2 Think about what bad habits you have right now. Are you watching too much TV or spending too much time scrolling social media? Use a screen time app on your phone to limit your time on the phone and apps so you can be more productive. Use this time to work on the habits you want to cultivate. Remember create more and consume less.

Pick habits to work on for seven days straight and see which ones stick and then hold on to them. That's how you build great habits for the long term.

15

PLAYING THE GAME OF LIFE

NEW! Level 15
acquired!

Complete

"**Most people overestimate what they can do in one year and underestimate what they can do in ten years.**"

LIFE IS PRETTY SIMPLE: it's just a series of levels to beat. In almost any game, you start out with nothing. No money, no armor, no weapons, no friends. You have to work your way up. On your way up, you encounter obstacles. People are mean. Competitors try to hold you back. Your friends alienate you for aiming for the stars. And that's okay. A chip on your shoulder can be a great motivator.

As you become more proficient at your craft, you begin to set yourself apart from others. That's when other people start to gravitate toward you. Why? Because you add value to their lives. They know that you will make their lives better. The more useful you become to the world, the more people will be pulled toward you.

Smart hard work is something that anyone can do. Most of the time, the people who have earned the most money in the world are also the ones who have provided the most value and worked the hardest. Elon Musk said that "you get paid in direct proportion to the difficulty of problems you solve." Feel free to disagree with me, but I'm a firm believer that anyone who works hard to provide value will eventually achieve success.

But life is never a straight line to the top. You'll face incredibly difficult trials along the way. Time spent with your loved ones will be sacrificed. Outside circumstances will block you from accomplishing things you've always wanted to do. As the world evolves, you'll have to constantly reinvent yourself or be left behind. And the list goes on.

What you can do to ensure your long-term success is to cultivate lasting habits and be willing to play the game of patience. Every overnight success takes years or decades to achieve.

Take Netflix for example:

- **Level 1:** They rented DVDs by mail. People paid per rental. It was a failing business model.

- **Level 2:** They rented DVDs by mail. People paid a monthly subscription. The business model worked because of the payment model switch.

- **Level 3:** They switched to streaming media online. The business exploded.

- **Level 4:** They went into original content production. Their userbase grew.

It took Netflix years to reach its current business model that the world now knows and loves. Netflix almost died in its early years and had to level up a few times by making critical adjustments in order to emerge from the arena victorious.

Take It to the Next Level

Now that you understand that life is a series of levels for you to conquer, it's time to talk about where to go next. Remember each level you defeat unlocks a new level of challenges for you to overcome. It is up to you whether you want to face those challenges or not. If you do, you will get to move to the next level. Then the next. Then the next. And so on.

So, when do the levels end? The answer is they really don't. It is your decision if you want to continue leveling up in certain areas of your life. Life gamification is about continually challenging yourself and adding new power-ups to help you reach your long-term goals.

If you want to push hard on your career and then open a new quest of having a family, that's perfectly fine. Just understand that your progression on the career level will slow significantly until you can dedicate more time and energy into it. It's hard enough to try to defeat one boss by yourself. Two is much harder.

I learned about the four burners theory from bestselling author James Clear. The four "burners" in your life are:

1 Health
2 Family
3 Friends
4 Work

Those are the four games you can play in life. We are all limited to the same twenty-four hours in a day so we are not able to play all four games simultaneously to the best of our abilities. There's just not enough time. So, you must choose the game at which you want to excel.

Didn't see this coming? The last level always includes difficult choices! Life is a game filled with trade-offs and if you want to play at an elite level, you have to make sacrifices. If you want to balance all four games all the time, that's fine to try, too—but you won't ever realize your full potential in any one game because your attention is split.

Life gamification is about **continually challenging yourself.**

There are some ways to cope with managing the four burners:

1 You can hire someone to assist you with some of the burners.

2 You can decide to completely focus on certain burners while sacrificing others. Then you can pick up the other ones later. For example, if you want to be exceptional at business, you may decide to sacrifice time with friends. Then when you become successful in business, you might dial down the work intensity and spend more time with your friends.

3 You can set time constraints each day on how long you focus on each burner.

The important thing is that you be intentional about how you spend your time. Do this, and you'll reap the long-term benefits of your focus and efforts.

Don't Ever Stop Collecting Power-Ups

One more thing: the power-ups in this book are just the starting point for you. There are many more power-ups to collect as your journey continues.

Where do you find these power-ups? For starters, you need to continue to study the habits and routines of the individuals mentioned in this book if you want to get better. You can start by reading their biographies. Look for other entrepreneurs to study. Entrepreneurs are often the biggest thinkers who challenge the status quo. *Everything* around you was built by an entrepreneur of some sort. Entrepreneurs aren't necessarily businesspeople; they may be creators—artists, musicians, designers, and so on.

The One Concept You Need to Understand: The Ladders of Wealth Creation

Everyone has a different path in life, but there's no skipping levels. You always have to beat one level in order to unlock the next. If you fail, you will stay where you are until you make it a priority to level up.

Here's what levels might look like in a romantic relationship:

- **Level 1:** You are single.
- **Level 2:** You go out on dates.
- **Level 3:** You get into a relationship.
- **Level 4:** You get married.
- **Level 5:** You have children.

Here's what career levels look like for some people:

- **Level 1:** Go to school.
- **Level 2:** Master a skill.
- **Level 3:** Work for someone.
- **Level 4:** Start a business.
- **Level 5:** Buy other businesses.

Let's say you get past level 1—go to school—but you stop there and do not master a skill. That limits your career options: you need skills to provide value to an employer. You will be stuck at this level until you build a skill. On the flip side, if you do well as a business owner and pass level 4, you are incentivized to continue to invest and take risks. At level 5, you might buy or build other businesses.

Here are the career progressions I went through. I'm no different than you, and if I can do it, you can do it, too!

1 Data entry job
2 Marketing internship
3 Marketing manager
4 SEO manager
5 SEO strategist
6 VP of marketing
7 COO of marketing agency
8 CEO of marketing agency
9 CEO of software company; hired CEO for marketing agency
10 Investor, founder, podcaster

The following illustration is of the levels of wealth creation. Take a hard look to identify where you are on the ladders. It will give you a good idea of what you need to do to advance to the next level.

Leveling up is a fundamental life game that we all play as human beings. The ones who are constantly leveling up are the ones who see the most success. Remember if you're not growing, you're dying.

For me, the most rewarding game to play in life is the great game of business. Because you are ultimately responsible for your own success, you have uncapped potential; you can build a team based on your vision, and you can creatively use your business to propel your biggest ideas. Owning a business gives you the most leverage since your equity can be worth a fortune. What's more important is that you can make the impact that you want to make—you can create the change that you want to see.

THE LADDERS OF WEALTH CREATION

Every career starts in the bottom left and works through each ladder over time. The higher you climb, the more you earn, but the more skills and experience you need to acquire.

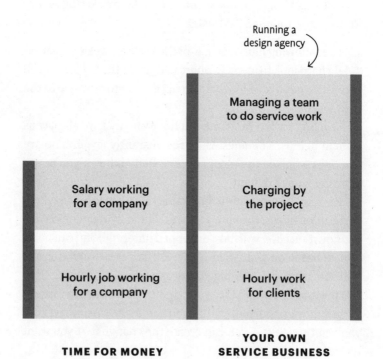

Running a design agency

Managing a team to do service work

Salary working for a company

Charging by the project

Hourly job working for a company

Hourly work for clients

TIME FOR MONEY

YOUR OWN SERVICE BUSINESS

Facebook, Uber, & eBay

Marketplaces &
social networks

Editing up to four videos
for $ 1,000 per month

SaaS
(Software as a Service)

Recurring
productized services

Subscription software
launched with
consulting services

Recurring services
provided by employees

Physical products
& commerce

Selling consulting
packages

Products sold in an
existing ecosystem
(iOS apps, WordPress
plugins, & Airbnb houses)

Fixed scope for
a fixed price

Digital products
(ebooks, courses,
& downloadables)

PRODUCTIZED SERVICES   **SELLING PRODUCTS**

If you want to print out this image, go to LevelingUp.com.

Beginning Your Journey

A final piece of advice before you conquer the world: we are *all* at different chapters in our lives. It's easy to compare yourself to others and think you're inferior. You're not. You might be at your level 1 while somebody else is at their level 25. *Everybody* is fighting a different battle at a different stage. Always remember that and don't be too hard on yourself—or others. You never know what opponent someone else is facing.

Now go forth, level up, and win at the game of life!

Achievement unlocked!

Congratulations on reaching the end of the book! You have unlocked the **GAMER** framework.

- **Get reading:** Never stop growing and learning.
- **Alchemy:** Sales and marketing will play in a role throughout your entire life. Master them.
- **Meditation:** Control what you can control. Nothing else matters.
- **Endurance:** Stay patient and be resilient in the face of adversity.
- **Repetition:** There's no champion in the world who hasn't honed their craft over and over. Build the right routines and repeat them over and over!

I narrowed it down to this memorable framework because starting with these five power-ups will help you continue to reinforce good habits and refine and build more power-ups throughout your life. Whenever you're feeling lost, come back to the GAMER framework for guidance.

Take the passcode numbers you got from entering in codes at **levels 4, 8, 10, 12,** and **14** and go to **LevelingUp.com/bonus-complete** to get the bonus and a special video from me. What *is* the bonus? Let's just say it will help you cultivate the power-ups you need to build the life of your dreams.

ACKNOWLEDGMENTS

ALTHOUGH I'VE BEEN working on this book for the last five years of my life, the reality is I have been working on it throughout my entire journey on this world. I couldn't have gotten this done without all the encouragement and support from people all around me.

I'd like to thank my loyal podcast fans for lending me your ears since 2013.

A big thank-you to my team for continuing to work hard to help make my vision a reality.

To all my customers who took a shot and believed in us, thank you.

A massive thank-you to the Page Two team for making this book exceptional and guiding me through the process. I'm truly proud of the product.

To my friends and family who supported me throughout my journey and pushed me to finish this book.

And for anyone that I might have missed, thank you, thank you, thank you.

TOMB OF KNOWLEDGE

Recommended Books

- *Antifragile* by Nassim Nicholas Taleb
- *Breakthrough Advertising* by Eugene M. Schwartz
- *The Goal* by Eliyahu M. Goldratt
- *The Hard Thing About Hard Things* by Ben Horowitz
- *The Ideal Team Player* by Patrick Lencioni
- *Influence* by Robert Cialdini
- *Linchpin* by Seth Godin
- *Multipliers* by Greg McKeown and Liz Wiseman
- *The ONE Thing* by Gary W. Keller and Jay Papasan
- *The Talent Code* by Daniel Coyle
- *Traffic Secrets* and *DotCom Secrets* by Russell Brunson
- *Tribal Leadership* by Dave Logan and John King

Resources to Build an Online Business

- Asana for project management
- DreamHost for web hosting
- Google Drive for file collaboration

- HubSpot for CRM
- Libsyn for podcast hosting
- Loom for screencasts
- Mixmax for scheduling email sequences and finding the right time to email people
- Notion for online wiki
- 1Password for password management
- Slack for online chat
- Ubersuggest for free SEO software
- WordPress for content management system
- Zoom for online conferencing

Educational Podcasts

- *a16z*
- *Indie Hackers*
- *Leveling Up*
- *Marketing School*
- *Smart Passive Income*

Health Resources

- Calm or Headspace for meditation
- Oura Ring for sleep tracking

Eric's Favorite Tools

- Alfred to quickly pull up files in MacOS
- Nuzzel to aggregate top retweeted content from Twitter followers
- Overcast for listening to podcasts
- Pocket for saving content to read later
- TextExpander for accessing frequently used snippets of text
- Video Speed Controller plugin for Chrome to increase video speed

ABOUT
THE AUTHOR

ERIC SIU is an investor, founder, and advisor. He has
helped companies such as Amazon, Airbnb, Uber, and
Salesforce through his ad agency, Single Grain. He also
hosts two podcasts, *Marketing School* and *Leveling Up*,
where he talks about personal and business growth. Combined, the podcasts have over thirty-five million downloads.
In his youth, Eric was not academically or socially successful,
but he thrived in eSports and poker. He ultimately found how
to convert his focus and accolades in gaming into business
success and wants to help others do the same. His life mission
is to help the world level up.

HELP ME LEVEL UP!

DID YOU LEARN ANYTHING valuable from *Leveling Up*? If so, I'd be eternally grateful if you could help me by taking action and doing any of the following:

1 Give this book a **five-star review** on your favorite online retailer. Every review goes a long way!

2 Go to **LevelingUp.com** and subscribe to the email list for more goodies and learnings.

3 Follow me on Instagram at **@ericosiu**.

4 Follow me on Twitter at **@ericosiu**.

5 Subscribe to my YouTube channel at **YouTube.com/c/Growth Everywhere**.

6 Subscribe to the ***Leveling Up* podcast** on your favorite podcast platform.